The Path of Duty

The Wartime Letters of
Alwyn Bramley-Moore
1914-1916

The Path of Duty

The Wartime Letters of
Alwyn Bramley-Moore
1914-1916
(03 July 1878 – 04 April 1916)

Edited and with Introduction by
Ken Tingley

Published by
Alberta Records Publication Board
HISTORICAL SOCIETY OF ALBERTA
General Editors: David W. Leonard and David C. Jones, 1998
Volume XI

Copyright © 1997
Historical Society of Alberta
Box 4035, Station C
Calgary, Alberta
T2T 5M9

All rights reserved

Canadian Cataloguing in Publication Data

Bramley-Moore, Alwyn, 1878-1916
   The path of duty

Includes index.
Copublished by: Alberta Records Publication Board
ISBN 1-55056-567-2

   1. Bramley-Moore, Alwyn, 1878-1916--Correspondence. 2. World War, 1914-1918--Personal narratives, Canadian. 3. Soldiers--Canada--Correspondence. I. Tingley, Kenneth W. (Kenneth Wayne), 1947- II. Historical Society of Alberta. III. Alberta Records Publication Board. IV. Title
D640.B735 1998   940.54'8171   C98-910074-X

First printing 1998

Cover art: Oil on canvass, *A. Bramley-Moore* (no date) by Sir Edmund Wyley Grier (1862-1957) from the collection of the Government of Alberta (catalogue No. 0410. 3000. 000048)

Printed and bound in Canada by   Friesens Corporation
                                                Altona, Manitoba, Canada

CONTENTS

Preface:
Countess Mountbatten of Burma, Colonel-in-Chief,
Princess Patricia's Canadian Light Infantry iv

Dedication v

Acknowledgments.. vi

Introduction... viii

Notes on Editing... xxii

The Wartime Letters of
Alwyn Bramley-Moore 1914-1916 1

I.   In England With the Royal Fusiliers.................. 1

II.   With The Princess Patricia's
     Canadian Light Infantry.......................... 51

Epilogue 129

Biographical Afterword 130

Endnotes 133

Index 136

PREFACE

This remarkable series of letters written to his children at home in Canada by Lance Corporal Alwyn Bramley-Moore from England and France in 1914-1916, gives us an unusual insight into the life of a soldier of "The Great War."

Bramley-Moore volunteered, as did so many countless other men, to "join up" and go overseas to fight at the outbreak of war. He felt very strongly that as an Englishman originally, he owed it to his old homeland to do so. However, in his letters to his young family, he frequently impresses upon them that Canada - and especially Alberta, where they live - is a great and expanding country, and they should grow up especially proud to be Albertans. His letters are full of the advice and interest in their welfare that a caring father would feel, despite the thousands of miles and many long months that separate them. He is obviously a well-educated man who loves and values his books and wishes his children to do the same. They are encouraged to work hard at school, be brave and stalwart and loyal, as well as caring and supportive to each other and their mother.

We read of the endless months of drilling, route marching and general training in England, until finally he and his fellow soldiers reach the Front Line in the trenches in France. He keeps a brave face on the hardships endured there for his family's sake, but it is not difficult to imagine how terrible those conditions must have been. After six months of ghastly warfare this middle-aged, family man (longing to see his children grow up) is killed by a sniper's bullet.

Alwyn Bramley-Moore started his wartime service with the Royal Fusiliers (11th) but later transferred to the Princess Patricia's Canadian Light Infantry. As Colonel-in-Chief of that very fine Regiment I am very pleased to be associated with this straightforward, thoughtful account of a First World War "Patricia," and the fine example of loyal service to this country which he sets us.

Countess Mountbatten of Burma
Colonel-in-Chief
Princess Patricia's Canadian Light Infantry

DEDICATION

To Nelly Bramley-Moore, who encouraged her children not only to preserve their father's letters, but also to live as he hoped they would; to Laura Bramley-Moore, his eldest daughter, who started the collation of the letters for publication; and to the Bramley-Moore family for generously sharing the letters that detail Alwyn Bramley-Moore's unique experience of the First World War.

ACKNOWLEDGEMENTS

I would like to offer my sincere thanks to the Rt. Hon. Countess Mountbatten of Burma, Colonel-in-Chief, Princess Patricia's Canadian Light Infantry, for her interest and support, as well as for the preface written for this collection of letters.

The Bramley-Moore family has been very helpful in assembling the letters held by several of its widely scattered members. It was initially Miss Laura Bramley-Moore who contacted me to edit and annotate these letters. After Laura's death, Gladys Bramley-Moore continued her sister's project. The resulting publication was planned during several very pleasant meetings at their home in Victoria, British Columbia. Helen Sanderson, who posesses many of the original letters, provided invaluable inspiration and assistance to Laura during the ordering and typing the letters. Alan Coulter and his family, of Saskatoon, provided the complete letters written to his father-in-law Alfred. Mary Anne Kinloch, who now owns the Bramley-Moore quilt mentioned in the letters, loaned it to us so that it could be photographed. Unless otherwise noted, all photographs were provided by the Bramley-Moore family.

The Princess Patricia's Canadian Light Infantry Museum, at the Museum of the Regiments in Calgary, has supported this project enthusiastically. In particular, Regimental Major John T. McComber, C.D., Sergeant Mark Atwood, and Marie-Anne Brothers opened their archival collections to me, and added their insights into the history of their Regiment. The Heritage Committee of the P.P.C.L.I. Association provided funds for the reproduction of the portrait of Alwyn Bramley-Moore on the front cover.

Patricia Walker conducted archival research in England, locating and verifying details of Alwyn Bramley-Moore's early years before his immigration to Canada in 1895. My thanks to Charles Bazalgette for his assistance in England as well.

Timothy D. Dubé, Military Archivist in the Manuscript Division at the National Archives of Canada, directed me to several important sources. These include the Agar Adamson letters, portraying an officer's viewpoint of the Patricias during the period when Alwyn Bramley-Moore served with that Regiment. His advice and encouragement during my research in Ottawa was invaluable.

In Edmonton, Danial Duda helped at the University of Alberta Library and provided maps; Brock Silversides meticulously prepared negatives and prints of the family photographs and souvenirs as well as the colour transparency for the cover portrait; Betty Rothwell, Registrar for the Alberta Art Collection, made the cover portrait available; Mr. Moses Jung, Executive Assistant to the Speaker, Legislature of Alberta, approved use of the cover portrait; Maurice Doll, Curator of Government History at the Provincial Museum of Alberta, read the manuscript and clarified the military context; Barbara Dacks, editor of *Legacy: Alberta's Heritage Magazine*, allowed me to use material first printed in the Winter 1996 issue; Miss Alison Seymour and Ms. Michelle DeAbreu advised me during translation of the French *pensées* in Letter 85; and David Leonard and David Jones gave their encouragement and editorial suggestions.

Thanks to Gerald and June Klassen, Barbara Klassen, and Harold and Erma Klassen in Saanich, British Columbia, for their support; and of course, my wife, Sheila, who accompanied me and participated in much of the research.

Alwyn Bramley-Moore, Member of the Alberta Provincial Parliament, Alexandra Constituency, 1909-1913

INTRODUCTION: "ALBERTA, FIRST, LAST AND FOREVER."

Lance Corporal Alwyn Bramley-Moore was shot by a German sniper on a cold night in late March 1916. When he died on 4 April in the No. 13 General Hospital in Boulogne, his passing went generally unremarked in the broader disaster of the Great War. However, unknown to most of his comrades in the Princess Patricia's Canadian Light Infantry, this middle-aged Englishman had already made a mark in his adopted country of Canada. By 1916, he had been a homesteader, entrepreneur, writer, Member of the Provincial Parliament in Alberta, outspoken freethinker, and possibly Alberta's first "sovereigntist." Alwyn was also the father of five children, and, during his wartime absence, wrote to them all warmly, humourously, sometimes pedantically, but always as their "affectionate father." These letters, written from November 1914 until March 1916, form a valuable historical record of one of the province's earliest parliamentarians.

In 1911, Alwyn wrote in *Canada and Her Colonies, or Home Rule for Alberta*, that he believed in "Alberta, first, last and forever." Although his transformation from an Englishman to a Canadian and an Albertan was virtually complete, when war was declared in August 1914, he still felt profound ties to the country of his birth and upbringing, like so many English Canadians of his generation. He wrote from England to his son, Alfred:

> I hope you will grow up to be a good Albertan; Alberta is a big enough country to be proud of and you children have grown up with it and should look upon it as your land. I was born here, so this country has claims on me but if I pay those claims then you won't owe them.[1]

When word of his death reached Edmonton, Alwyn was mourned by friends and colleagues. Edmonton, the provincial capital, was still a small city in which the social and political leaders knew each other well. Premier A.L. Sifton commissioned a portrait of the former Liberal Member of the Provincial Parliament, and it hung for many years outside the Assembly in the Alberta Legislature in Edmonton.

A. Balmer Watt, editor of the *Edmonton Journal*, and a close friend, eulogized him in his newspaper. The Edmonton *Bulletin* announced his death on 12 April, 1916. The next day it reported that 944 westerners had been killed or wounded at St. Eloi. Life on the home front had become a weary litany of destruction in which the death of one man seemed to pale amid the stories of mass slaughter.

Alwyn Bramley-Moore was born on 3 July, 1878 at 19 Woburn Square in Bloomsbury, London. His father, William Joseph, was a clerk in orders at the time; his mother was Ella Bradshaw Jordan. In the 1881 Census, Alwyn's father indicated that he was a "Minister of the Catholic Apostolic Church." Alwyn was the eleventh of fourteen children, all apparently born in Bloomsbury. Miss Martha M. Wriede, a young German governess from Altona, was living with the Bramley-Moore family by 1881, and the children appear to have been privately tutored. Jemima Hornewood was their domestic servant in the 1880s, while a "visitor" named Elizabeth Curtis, an unmarried woman of 29, was living with the household. By Alwyn's teens, the family had moved to 26 Russell Square, also in Bloomsbury. At the time of the 1891 Census, the household had grown to include Miss Jane E. Cutler, a 27-year-old governess, as well as a cook, housemaid, parlour maid, kitchen maid and footman.[2]

William Joseph Bramley-Moore was born on 27 August, 1831 in Rio de Janiero, Brazil, and Ella Bradshaw was born there in 1844. After moving to England, The Rev. Bramley-Moore was the first minister at Langley Lodge, Gerrards Cross, in Buckinghamshire. He and his brother, A.J. Bramley-Moore, were noted for their "acts of kindness and charity...." They bequeathed the bells and clock in the tower in memory of their father, John Bramley-Moore, who had built a famous well near the crossroads of Windsor and Oxford Roads. The well still survives, with an inscription reading, "This pump was erected by John Bramley-Moore, Esq., M.P., in the year 1864 for the use of the wayfarer in Gerrards Cross. 'Whoever will let him take of the water of life freely.'" The Rev. Bramley-Moore died on 5 October, 1918.[3]

Like many young Englishmen of the time, Alwyn immigrated to Canada, the land of fresh promise promoted everywhere in England by the federal government and the Canadian Pacific Railway. He was 17 when he arrived in the Dominion in 1895, where he established himself in the Sombra district, near Sarnia, Ontario. In 1899, he married Nellie Grieve, and they established their own farm.

In 1903, he and his wife moved west to the Northwest Territories, arriving in Saskatoon early that year. There he met the Barr Colonists, who were preparing for the trip west to what would soon be known as the Lloydminster area.⁴ The Bramley-Moores travelled from Saskatoon to the Barr Colony with this group, living in wagons and sharing in the hardships of that poorly planned enterprise.

In 1906, Toronto *Globe* reporter Fred A. Acland visited Lloydminster and reported that even "the few of the newcomers who had farmed in England found themselves strangers to the soil of the prairie and had to learn their methods anew, though for the moment there were none from whom to learn."⁵ Acland observed that between 1903 and 1906, almost 15,000 homesteads had been entered in the district. The majority were taken by English immigrants. Before the arrival of the Canadian Northern Railway in 1906, supplies were shipped down the North Saskatchewan River from Edmonton on barges. Despite problems, Acland concluded that they "have been woven quickly into the web of Canadian life, and are recognized on all sides as excellent settlers once they learn the methods of the new land. None are dissatisfied, and practically none would go back to England." Finally, he noted that these English homesteaders "were the real pioneers in a district which it is confidently predicted will show in the census taken last week, a population sufficient to elect a new member of parliament. Three years ago the coyote and the antelope had the land to themselves." ⁶

Alwyn Bramley-Moore, seen in the centre of this photograph, prepares to run the "official's race" at the Lloydminster Sports Day, about three months after his election in Alexandra Constituency

In 1909, the Provincial Constituency of Vermilion was subdivided to accommodate this growing population. By this time, Alwyn had made a sufficient impact upon the people of the new Alexandra Constituency, and had so distinguished himself among the British pioneers who had settled there that he was elected to represent them in the second provincial election on 22 March, 1909. As the Liberal candidate, he carried the party flag for Alberta's first premier, Alexander C. Rutherford, and remained a Rutherford loyalist throughout his term in office, even during the divisive railway scandal.

The Alberta and Great Waterways Railway controversy would dominate Alberta politics during 1910, and Alwyn was in the thick of the fray. A major railway project had been one of the most important planks in the Liberal election platform in the previous year. This railway company was incorporated to open up and develop northern Alberta by building a line from Edmonton to Fort McMurray by way of Lac la Biche. Legislation passed in the 1909 Session allowed the government to guarantee company bonds for 350 miles at $20,000 per mile, as well as provide $400,000 for the Edmonton terminal. The agreement between the government and the A. and G.W. Company was signed on 7 October 1909; an Order-in-Council approving the agreement was passed soon after.

When Premier Rutherford announced in November that J. Pierpont Morgan and Company had sold the Alberta railway bond on the London market for a 10 percent commission, a political crisis began to build among "insurgents" within the Liberal Party. Many felt that the interests of the provincial taxpayers had been betrayed through poor financial planning for the railway. William H. Cushing, Minister of Public Works, soon resigned over the issue, and J.R. Boyle, M.P.P. for Sturgeon, openly attacked the agreement on 21 February 1910, with a critical preamble to his notice of a resolution to expropriate the assets of the railway company and continue the work through a government commission. During these debates, Alwyn continued to speak passionately in defence of the agreement.[7]

Shortly after this, R.B. Bennett led the Conservative opposition charge against the government ranks with a spirited speech before a crowded visitors' gallery in the Legislature, attacking the laxness of the government in allowing speculators to use Alberta money for their own profits. Amid growing dissatisfaction within and outside the party, a Royal Commission was called to investigate charges of corruption. During the commission hearings, public confidence in

Rutherford failed, and, on 26 May, 1910 he resigned under party pressure. Arthur L. Sifton, Chief Justice of Alberta since 1907, was then appointed Premier by Lieutenant-Governor George H.V. Bulyea. It was hoped that Sifton, as a non-partisan, could heal the rift in the party.

Throughout the debate, Alwyn had remained loyal, even though most Liberals turned against Rutherford. Alwyn saw the real root of the problem faced by the government as lack of control in developing the province's own resources. He felt this had caused the situation that resulted in the scandal, and, in November, he introduced a motion supporting efforts to secure provincial control of natural resources. As late as 14 December 1910, he introduced a motion asking that the Provincial Parliament vote its confidence in the integrity of the former government following the findings of the Royal Commission, which cast doubt on its competence, but failed to find evidence of corruption. The Speaker ruled the motion out of order, and Rutherford stated that he would stand by his record. It was an awkward moment for Rutherford, as well as Alwyn.[8]

In 1910, Alwyn moved his family to Edmonton, and took up residence at 624 Hardisty Avenue. Members of his family would continue to live in this house until 1962. With his residence located near the Provincial Parliament Building, he numbered among his

The Bramley-Moore family and friends on the verandah of their Edmonton home just before World War 1.

neighbours J.R. Boyle, like himself a prominent participant in the railways dispute.

During the dispute, Alwyn became convinced that the only effective way for Alberta to direct the development of its resources was to gain control of those resources, which had been retained by the federal government when the province was created in 1905. In November 1910, he introduced a motion committing the provincial government to petition the Laurier government to transfer control of Crown land and natural resources. Premier Sifton remained lukewarm, and asked Alwyn to withdraw the motion. More inclined to support a negotiated pursuit of this goal, Sifton and many other Members did not want to sound too critical of the senior government in Ottawa, which was also Liberal and included Edmonton's Frank Oliver as Minister of the Interior. However, an amended resolution was passed unanimously, and committed Alberta to the long road which would finally culminate in 1930 with the transfer of natural resources envisioned by Alwyn.[9]

Shortly after the collapse of the Rutherford administration, Alwyn wrote the book for which he is most remembered. *Canada and Her Colonies, or Home Rule for Alberta* was published in 1911 and addressed all of the issues which he had confronted during his first two years as a Member of the Provincial Parliament. In this book, he wrote that Rutherford's government was brought down through "the total overthrow of their efforts to open up the northern portions of the province." As Alwyn saw it, the problem which had shaken Alberta to its political foundations was its "colonial" relationship to central Canada:

> Nothing could have more forcibly brought home to my mind the injustice of a state of affairs by which a Provincial Government assumes the liabilities incident to the development of a vast country while the natural resources of that country are owned and controlled by a foreign Government.

In this case, the foreign government was Ottawa. As he concluded, Alberta had merely tried to build a railway "into regions where every square inch of land, every stick of timber, every pound of mineral belonged to the Dominion Government."[10]

Alwyn criticized the limitations of what he called the "provincial constitution," concluding that Alberta "must own her own natural resources, be they lands, minerals or timber." This fight would take another two decades to win, and he would be long dead when the province would finally achieve the goal in 1930. However, he was one of the first to define the problem systematically, and to forge the rhetoric for an ideology of oppression which would last for years in the fight for a fair shake from Ottawa. In fact, in June 1980, while Alberta was embroiled in the constitutional and energy wars with Ottawa, the *Edmonton Journal* reprinted excerpts from the book, concluding that "he foresees the very political struggles unfolding this month as Alberta and Ottawa seek a new energy agreement, and as the first ministers gather for a constitutional conference."[11]

Having come to Canada as a young man, Alwyn felt the excitement of living in a new province, and wrote of his pride in Alberta and his faith in its people. In fact, he identified immediately with his fellow Albertans, and wrote in his book that "a nation endowed with such qualities will never for any length of time endure a curtailment of national rights incompatible with a proper self-respect." He argued that western Canada had not consented to its inclusion in the Dominion following its acquisition from the Hudson's Bay Company, and concluded that the western "colonies" had been obtained through purchase, war (the Northwest Rebellion), and occupation. All the other provinces had "voluntarily entered into a partnership with the exception of the North-West Territories." Canada, on the other hand, regarded the West merely as "lands acquired by herself as a speculation or an investment", and looked upon herself as "a veritable fairy godmother heaping priceless treasures on some lucky orphan."

Canada and Her Colonies drew upon a comparison with "the Irish problem." Alwyn recalled that the Canadian House of Commons had passed resolutions in 1882 recommending Home Rule for Ireland, but now he compared Alberta unfavourably to Ireland with respect to representation in the national parliament, influence in national affairs and distance from the centre of government. Bramley-Moore complained that, despite some representation in Ottawa, Alberta had "not the slightest control" over federal policy:

> Of what account are seven members among two hundred? Any influence they could exert would be infinitesimal. A 3 1/2 per cent. solution may be efficacious in medical practice, but in the arena of the political conflict its effect is nil.

Finally, he wrote that "very little thought should convince Sir Wilfrid [*Laurier*] that Irish grievances stand on a far weaker footing than Albertan grievances." Ironically, Alwyn was killed while serving with the Princess Patricia's Canadian Light Infantry less than a month before the Easter Rising in Dublin was crushed by the British government.

Like later separatists, Alwyn assumed a technocratic tone in his writing, using the vocabulary of the social sciences to bolster his arguments. "History is a science if properly viewed," he declared, giving an air of inevitability to the emerging Alberta "nationhood." His book is discursive at times, and its global scale sometimes suggested the approach taken by H.G. Wells and other popular historians of the time. Like Wells, he detected "the great (organic) principle of sub-division" at work in the world, adding to the sense of predetermination in developing nation-states: "From a geographical standpoint there is no more sense in a union between Alberta and Eastern Canada than there is between Eastern Canada and England." And, like later separatists, Alwyn looked to the example of Norway leaving Sweden, and concluded that, in the modern world, "the idea of a war for the purpose of forcing a race into an unwilling union is abhorrent."

After describing the "spoliation of western lands by the Dominion," he concluded that "It remains to be seen whether Western Canadians have lost the spirit of their fathers." Perhaps inconsistenly, he felt that the best way to accommodate this spirit of independence lay in Canadian imperial ties with Britain. The answer was to take Alberta's grievances to the Imperial Parliament in London, in order that the province might be made an equal and distinct part of the British Empire:

> A radical procedure, and rather a practical one in its way, would be to hoist the flag of independence, which would *ipso facto* make the province owner of her own resources. After a banquet or two and patriotic oratory, the province might express a desire to be reinstated in the Confederation, and then she would be in a position to make a bargain.

He ended his book with the statement that he was not urging secession from Canada, but this could well happen unless changes were made:

Is Canada prepared to hold Alberta with or without her will? Does she imagine that she will have the same good fortune as attended the Northern States when they coerced the Southern Confederacy? The cases are very different, though the results would have been the same in both instances if Richmond, like Edmonton, had been separated from Washington by a vast stretch of wilderness.[12]

Concluding that Sir Wilfrid Laurier's proclamation, "Canada first, last and forever," had not prejudiced the Dominion's imperial ties, Alwyn felt that "no disrespect to Confederation is implied when the citizens of Alberta take for their motto: "Alberta first, last and forever."[13]

Alwyn's expressed political views were not confined to Alberta; indeed, he was intensely interested in many other intellectual issues of his time. While in Edmonton he wrote a manuscript on marriage and sexual morals. Its rationalist tone and arguments are similar to those of Beatrice Webb, the socialist economist and a founder of the Fabian Society. It is also reminiscent of Bertrand Russell's *Marriage and Morals* (1929), which would still shock and outrage its North American readers almost two decades later. Alwyn's manuscript concludes that "marriage customs of today have evolved from the marriage or mating habits of our ancestors. Their mating habits were formed unconsciously as a result of environment." He believed that a "science of sexual relations" could identify the cause of "the present system of monogamy which is nominally the one in vogue in Western civilization." With other writers, he identified St. Paul as the culprit in creating the sexual hysteria which identified women as a threat to morality, and led to the "distorted views" on the subject of many Christians:

> St. Paul's suspicions of the female sex can be seen even in those passages in which he tolerates them. As women formed part of the early congregations, it may appear surprising that they did not resent such cavalier treatment as was handed them by St. Paul. It must be remembered though, that the good Christian will even grow enthusiastic at the thought that he is a miserable sinner, and it is quite possible that the women enjoyed gloating over the lively portrayals of the wickedness of their sex as depicted by the early Fathers.[14]

Attacking the patriarchal system nurtured by religion, he noted that the Romans more logically "granted comparative freedom" to women:

> This freedom was lost when the sinister influence of Christianity usurped the place of logic and befuddled men's minds with absurd and childish superstitions. Once again in our own day woman commences to regain her proper position as man's equal....[15]

Alwyn's own view was that "Woman is not a devil, woman is not a piece of property, woman is not an angel, woman is a human being and should be treated as one."

Advocating "a more sensible marriage system," Alwyn concluded that:

> Man has been taught that he must conform his tastes to some arbitrary marriage customs. These marriage customs should have been altered to suit man's needs and tastes. Marriage should be an additional means to happiness; it has been made a principal source of wretchedness. For a little while we represent a certain combination of the molecules of matter. We should surely endeavour to render that little while as pleasant as possible and refrain from absurdities.[16]

His general critique of western sexual morals and institutions was fundamentally a critique of Christianity:

> The curse of Christianity still hampers modern civilization. Christianity *par excellence* insisted on the importance of the Unknowable and ever since it became the paramount religion, earthly motives have had to give place to heavenly guesses.

He concluded that "Christianity witnessed the triumph of superstition or faith over reason." Where Roman civilization was the product of reason, "the downfall of reason was equally the downfall of civilization." He slyly commented that "Christian historians innocently admit this by the epithet of 'Dark Ages' which they have assigned to the era in which Christianity held the preeminent position." While reason had again reasserted itself "in spite of the bitter and unceasing persecution of Christianity," Christianity "with its usual disregard for truth invariably claims the credit of modern civilization." Alwyn regarded this view as "astounding impudence!" In his opinion, the Dark Ages were "the offspring of Christianity; we are what we are today not owing to Christianity but in spite of Christianity." [17]

When his term in the Provincial Parliament ended in 1913, Alwyn declined to stand for re-election in Alexandra Constituency. N.C. Lyster carried the Liberal banner, but was narrowly defeated by J.R. Lowery.[18] It appears that Alwyn had become disillusioned with the internal fighting in the Liberal Party. Also, he had remained a loyalist, supporting the Rutherford government even during the 1913 campaign, and his loyalty may have cost him support from within the reorganized party. Still, he campaigned for the party, and addressed a political meeting in support of candidate William F. Puffer in Todd's Hall in Alix. There he "proceeded to enlighten the audience on a few of the leading questions of the day, his main theme being Alberta's Natural Resources."[19]

From the election of 17 April, 1913 until the outbreak of war in August 1914, Alwyn pursued several business ventures. As early as 1906, he had undertaken a type of entrepreneurial endeavour common to young and upcoming British immigrants during these boom

Alwyn Bramley-Moore accompanied Henry Marshall Tory on the banking and agricultural credit mission to Europe in 1913. Here they are shown with other delegates in Germany.

years. "An Act to Incorporate the Vermilion and Cold Lake Company" was given assent by the first provincial legislative session on 9 May, 1906. Alwyn's partners in this venture were Marshall Willard Hopkins, Surveyor, and Robert Wesley Ginn, a farmer from Lloydminster. Like many similar projects envisioned on paper during these years, this railway venture was never undertaken. From 1911 until his death, Alwyn also was vice-president of Battle River Collieries, which operated a coal mine about 3.5 miles east of Ohaton. His partners were A.S. Rosenroll, President, and C.T. Stacey, of Saskatoon, who was the managing director.[20]

When the war came in August 1914, he and his brother, Alfred, were on their regular fall canoe trip to Cold Lake. Hearing the news when they arrived there, they abandoned their canoes and hurried back to Edmonton. After a hasty farewell, Alwyn enlisted with the 11th Battalion, then being raised in Saskatchewan. Its mobilization depot was Camp Valcartier, but it later became the 11th Reserve Battalion, a training unit at Tidworth Barracks in England. Once in England, however, Alwyn made his way to St. Paul's Churchyard, where he enlisted into the Royal Fusiliers Regular Army and was posted to the 1st Sportsman's Battalion on 8 October, 1914. He listed his occupation as "broker" on his attestation paper at this time. Alwyn (now No.179) was promoted to the rank of Corporal on 19 March, 1915. By petitioning his old political adversary, R.B. Bennett, who was visiting England with Prime Minister Robert Borden in 1915, Alwyn was able to transfer to the Princess Patricia's Canadian Light Infantry on 7 September, 1915. He had been discharged from the Royal Fusiliers on Special War Office Instructions on 27 August, 1915, evidently through the intervention of Bennett. His letters make it clear that he wished to get more quickly to the front, and it was with the Patricias that Alwyn died after being wounded on the late night of 27 March, or early morning of 28 March, 1916.[21]

Alwyn's letters express the pride he felt in serving with his fellow Canadians. As Regimental Number 1834, his loyalties ran deepest with members of his section and platoon. While chafing at the idiocy of officers and useless drill, he never lost respect for the Regiment.

The Princess Patricia's Canadian Light Infantry, the most famous Canadian regiment of the Great War, was organized at Levis, Quebec on 10 August, 1914, under the direction of Major A. Hamilton Gault. Named for the daughter of the Governor General of Canada, it recruited among ex-soldiers for active service with the British Army, and was the first Canadian regiment to arrive in England, on 14 October. It was also the first to see action on the continent. The Patricias joined the 80th Brigade, 27th (British) Division on 16 November, and landed in France with that Division on 21 December, becoming the first unit of the formation to go into the trenches. The P.P.C.L.I. finally joined the Canadian Corps on 25 November, 1915 as part of the 7th Canadian Infantry Brigade, 3rd Canadian Division.[22]

Alwyn wrote regularly to his five children and his wife while serving overseas. These letters are interesting and valuable historical documents for several reasons. When he enlisted, he was approaching middle age, was well educated, a writer and former Member of the Provincial Parliament, used to exercising some authority. However, he rejected the pursuit of a commission, and chose to serve as a Private and Lance Corporal rather than as an officer. His letters are articulate and literate impressions of the war as seen by an enlisted man, filled with sardonic observations on the shortcomings of officers and politicians. His loyalties were almost equally divided between England and Canada. His letters reflect this fact as well.

What do his letters tell us about Alberta? They certainly provide insights into the kind of men who built the political and social foundations of a new province. Although far ahead of his time in some of his social theories, Alwyn was also quite typical in his belief in the Edwardian virtues of patriotism, hard work, and self-improvement. He was an educated person who valued the development of political ideas. He demonstrated, through his work as an M.P.P., and through his writing, how important he felt such values were in building Alberta. His communication of this feeling to his children indicated the depth of his commitment. He spoke in these letters of his love for England, and of his faith in Alberta. He urged his children to accept the duties of citizenship, but to commit their energies to Alberta, as he was "paying the debt" to England by his war service. He stressed the need to strike out and accept new ideas without abandoning core values, such as education and an open mind, and urged all his children, including his daughters, to follow these ideals. Through his family, Alwyn achieved the kind of influence he sought to bring to Alberta. His life and career also indicate the kind of men who, through their death on the battlefields of Europe during the Great War, were denied to the young province of Alberta during the postwar years, and the empty pages of history which their generation might have filled.

NOTES ON EDITING

Alwyn Bramley-Moore wrote his letters from England and France as personal correspondence to his five children. They were not meant for the public. Filled as they are with personal references, family jokes, and words of advice, they require some annotation in order to make them accessible to most readers. Alwyn was well educated and widely read, and his tastes reflected his class and time. Some of these references now require explanation.

In many ways, Alwyn was the perfect example of the ideal Edwardian father. His letters always urge the efficient use of time for self-improvement, and encourage his children to better themselves, even through their games. Such details add a significant dimension to the understanding of the man, and have been retained.

Many of the letters were written while Alwyn was cold, wet, hungry or exhausted. They therefore sometimes reveal small slips in grammar or spelling. These would have been corrected if the letters were intended for publication, and I have therefore done so for him. Several spellings of the period, although correct when written, are now obsolete and have been standardized in order to make them less intrusive for the reader. Conventions such as "&" were used by Alwyn to speed his writing and to conserve scarce paper. I have replaced them with "and." Punctuation was used sparingly in the original letters, but has been introduced where it sharpens the meaning. Several illegible words were referred to Gladys Bramley-Moore, who kindly helped to clarify them. Where uncertainty remains, I offer a best guess in square brackets; where words were dropped in haste, I have added them in square brackets. The censoring in letters 53 and 60 was done by military censors

No paragraphs were used in the letters, so I have introduced them to improve clarity and make the text read more fluently.

Footnotes and annotations identify personal references, and Alwyn's many literary allusions. Several other sources have been used to provide the military context. These include the War Diaries of the Princess Patricia's Canadian Light Infantry, the correspondence of Captain Agar Adamson (Second-in-Command, and Acting

Commanding Officer 4 June -3 August 1916, after Lt. Col. H.C. Buller was killed), and the correspondence of Major Stanley L. Jones. The War Diaries and Adamson Papers are held in the National Archives of Canada, while a copy of the correspondence of Major Jones and his wife is held by the P.P.C.L.I. Museum, Museum of the Regiments, Calgary. Since I consulted the Adamson letters at the National Archives of Canada, they have been published. (N. M. Christie, ed. *The Letters of Agar Adamson*. Nepean, Ontario: CEF Books, 1997)

Aside from these changes and annotations, almost all the letters from November 1914 until March 1916 are reproduced as written by Alwyn Bramley-Moore. These form a coherent and vital record of events in the trenches, and on the English home front. Even the mundane details capture the atmosphere of their time and place with an immediacy and colour which is otherwise impossible to convey.

Photo of Bramley-Moore children just before World War 1.

THE WARTIME LETTERS OF ALWYN BRAMLEY-MOORE 1914-1916

I. ENGLAND

LETTER 1
Nov. 2nd / 14
26 Russell Square[1]
London

Dear Dorothy:

I have just got one more day to stay here and then we are off to our camp in Essex where we will drill until we are fit to send off against the Germans. We will live in what they call "huts," but they must be large ones as 30 of us sleep in each hut. I have done a lot of marching but not much drilling yet.

You can write to this address now:
Private Bramley-Moore
179 No. 4 Company
Sportsman's Battalion
Hornchurch
Essex
England

179 is my regimental number.

I suppose it is starting to get cold with you. Tell your Mother that I want to know as soon as she starts getting the "separation allowance," and if there is any delay I can fix things up. The Government pays a "little" something for all of you children except Alfred; he is supposed to be big enough to get along without me!

I hope you children are able to play games without quarreling. I got Eva to post off four books to Alfred and William.[2] You should

---

[1] 26 Russell Square was the family home; it is now part of the University of London.

[2] Eva Bramley-Moore, who lived in Hove after the war, was a cousin of Alwyn Bramley-Moore's.

try to get somebody to read "Before Adam" aloud, as it is a nice story which I am sure you would all enjoy.[3]

I heard that Laura was 5th in her class, but I thought she stayed behind when the others were moved up. I shall expect you all to be very clever and learned when I get back. I haven't seen or heard of Mr. Johnson. It is too far to go where they are camped, tho' I believe some of them are over in Europe.

With love to all
    from your affectionate father
        A. B-M.

LETTER 2
DEC. 17th / 14
Hut 37, Sportsman's Battalion
Hornchurch, Essex

Dear William:

I have just received a letter from you for which many thanks. I have sent over several photos and you ought to have got them. I have just got an acknowledgement from Frank Walker at Fort Sask. for one I sent to him.[4]

You would have laughed if you had seen what happened to us the other day. It was wet and we were doing exercises in our hut. We have only privates in our hut and while the officer was there a corporal from some other hut came round and said he would drill us, but he was slightly drunk. At first we thought it might be funny but after awhile got tired of it. For here was this drunken corporal making us all run round and round the table!! It did look funny. But when he kept calling one of the men "a Leicestershire horse-dealer"

---

[3] *Before Adam* was a popular novel by Jack London, published in 1906; its narrator describes a series of connected dreams which apparently are regressive memories of "Big Tooth," an ancient progenitor who lived in the mid-Pleistocene era. His romantic tale describes how Big Tooth and his mate Swift One battle Red Eye and the Fire People, and the struggle for human survival during the distant past.

[4] Francis A. Walker represented the provincial Liberal Party in Victoria Constituency from 1905 until 1921. Lieutenant Walker was elected in 1917 in accordance with Chapter 38 of The Election Act, while serving overseas with the Canadian Expeditionary Force. He represented the Liberal Party in this constituency during the 1921 and 1926 provincial elections, but was defeated by the United Farmers of Alberta candidates.

in a sneering way the man at last turned on him and told him he wasn't going to be insulted by a drunk corporal whatever they might do to him, and we all backed him up, so the corporal stopped drilling us. The officer of course had gone before the row started.

I thought "Before Adam" a very good book. Did you like it? What did you think of "Red Eye?" I send you (with this letter) a cutting from the "Evening News" which may interest you and Alfred.

I daresay you have been told that I ought to have sheltered myself behind a woman's skirts instead of playing a man's part among men. Of course it is, as it ought to be, far pleasanter, if you are a man, playing a man's part, but because it is pleasanter that does not prove that one should have chosen the unpleasant job of just reading about battles instead of sharing in them. The Christians always imagine that it must be unpleasant to do your duty, and that if you are having a pleasant time, you must be wicked!! But I hope my boys will grow up with more sense, and will always have a smile whatever happens.

It won't be my fault if I don't get to the Front. I like my battalion immensely. We have had a lot of very nasty wet weather. This is a real war, my boy, and in a real war real men must take part, or "Red Eye" would run things just as he likes.

With love to all
    from your affectionate Father
        Alwyn Bramley-Moore

LETTER 3

Grey Towers Barracks
Hornchurch
Hut No. 37
[*20 January 1915*]

Dear William:

Many thanks for [*your*] letter. I have received too many papers; I like your letters but large bundles of newspapers are not worth sending; just cut out with the scissors what you think I would like to read. You have evidently been having some funny things happening in Edmonton.

I don't think that it matters at all what side god is on; first of course I don't believe there is one, and secondly, if there is and he thinks the Germans need beating because they are cruel, why trouble sending over so many Canadians, Australians etc.; couldn't god manage to lick them without getting all these other people killed. I don't think Kitchener or French trust in god, but they trust in big guns, lots of soldiers, good boots and clothes and food. And if we win we needn't thank god but we must thank all those who were either willing to go and fight or helped look after them. And you, my boy, when you grow up, you must learn to trust yourself and your friends; and if you learn well at school, then you will be able safely to trust yourself, but if you don't learn, trusting in god won't help you. When one wants help, one goes to one's friend, and if we are going to have friends, we must make ourselves pleasant and think about them as well as about ourselves and then when we need help - they are glad to help us; and if they are real friends, we can trust them. Don't make real friends with everybody, but when you make a real friend you must stick to him and not believe tales you hear.

I am kept busy digging trenches and drilling. I hope you like "Before Adam." I liked it. I may send some picture-cards in an envelope as they seem to get lost sometimes when I post them.

Lots of love to all and to yourself, my dear boy
from your affectionate Father
Alwyn

Post card sent to Laura from Romford. Her father wrote, "I saw this in a shop. I can't remember when it was taken but I think it must have been when we were having our lunch out trenching. Bully-beef, cheese and bread."

LETTER 4

Oct. 18th / 14
26 Russell Square

My dear Alfred:
I have been busy all week drilling. We march up and down the streets of London and go into the parks where we drill. We leave some time this week for our camp in the country.

I wonder if you could get some of that balsam gum and send it over to me; I want some especially as one's feet may get bruised or chafed in walking and I never saw anything better than that. Perhaps if everything is frozen, it may be impossible to get it.... There must be lots of spruce west from Edmonton. Do this if you can, as I would like some of the gum always with me. Also send me over the good pair of moccasins I bought, as they might be useful in camp. Send them to 26 Russell Square.

Be sure you study hard while you have the opportunity and try to play games without quarreling. There is no reason why you and the others shouldn't be able to play that card game we made without fighting.

Give my love to all the others.
From your affectionate Father
A. Bramley-Moore

LETTER 5

Grey Towers Barracks
Hornchurch
Hut No. 37

Dear Dorothy:
Many thanks for [the] letters. I like them from all of you.

Our battalion has a large band now so we hear a lot of tunes. Our regimental march is the "British Grenadiers." Get somebody to play it to you, and you will then know the tune we often march to. They always play it just as we enter the gate of our barrack after a march. I think it is a nice tune.

I let my moustache grow, so you would hardly recognize me in a photo now. It does seem to take a long time to make a soldier; they keep drilling and scolding and sometimes praising us. I think I walk a lot more upright now than I used to. It seems like being at school again. If we get back late or do something wrong, we are not allowed out of barracks. Now they blow a bugle every hour (they call it the defaulter's bugle) and you have to go and answer your name. They used not to do this, but now that they do nobody wants to become a defaulter.

On Saturday and Sunday afternoons, if we are not trenching, I and two or three chums walk to Romford, about two miles away, and go and have tea at a tea shop. You would think it a funny store; it is so small, and sometimes we have our tea in a small dining room where there is hardly room to move round, and sometimes, in the parlour upstairs. On Sundays the shop people use their own parlour, but they always ask us to come and sit as long as we like with them, and it is a pleasure to sit in easy chairs, as we only have forms to sit on in our huts.

I am glad you came first once. I will pay you your money sometime if I can. I don't get very big pay as a soldier. After deducting the 12 cts. a day I let them send home to you, I get about 75 cts. a week and my washing cost, 20 cts.; so unless I could borrow a little I would hardly be able to have tea at Romford.

I am glad I joined the Army because one likes to feel a man, and one might wonder if he was one if he let others do all the fighting, tho' of course all can't go. I try to write to all in turn.

Lots of love to all
    from your affectionate Father
        Alwyn

LETTER 6

Grey Towers Barrack
Hornchurch
[*10 November 1914*]

Dear Dorothy:

Many thanks for your letter which I got the other day. This is just like being at school again. Before breakfast we get physical exercises. We get up at 6:15 a.m. Then in the morning and afternoon we are drilled, and sometimes in the evening are taken out for a march. Yesterday I was cook's orderly, which means I had to go to the

Corporal Bramley-Moore (back row centre) with his company at Hornchurch.

cookhouse and wash potatoes, scrub tables and sinks and floors etc.

I am glad you are getting on with your work. I enclose a paper about our battalion. We are just off to drill so must close.

With love to all
    from your affectionate father
        A. B-M.

LETTER 7

26 Russell Square
W.C. (London)
12.11.14

Dear William:

I expect you'll be surprised to hear from me - but I thought you'd like to hear about your papa's march through London with his battalion. He looked very nice (that will please your Mother and the girls) in his uniform. The day they left for Hornchurch, Uncle Les and I went to see them parade in Hyde Park. Such crowds of people there - and two of the Royal Fusiliers' bands - great cheering after we saw them out of the park. Uncle Les walked by the band all the way to Liverpool Street. I took an omnibus and all along their route there were crowds of people, especially passing the Bank of

8   *England*

England and the Mansion House - the Lord Mayor and his party came out to the balcony. When we got to the station there was such a crowd I tried to get out of it - and got into a back part of the station, and accidentally came upon them again - they had a fine set-off.

Papa came up on Tuesday and looks very well. Tell your Mother he is very comfortable in his quarters, much more so than a good many Corps. I hope he won't go abroad until the Spring. Uncle John is here. He came back from France a week ago, and is waiting until he hears from the War Office where he is to go next.

Grandpa and Grandma are at Devon in Sidmouth.

Grandma is always so pleased when she hears from any of you.

Your Papa told me so many interesting things about you all.

My love to you all
> your afft.
> J.E. Cutler[5]

LETTER 8[6]

Grey Towers Barracks
Hornchurch
List "Hut 37" on left hand corner of envelope when writing. That is the number of my hut, it used to be 28 but changed.
Dec. 11th 1914

Dear Alfred:

I got your letter some days ago. I try to send a card to each in turn, but sometimes perhaps I make a mistake. I am always glad of your letters.

I can't give you any special information about the war from here, as we only hear things here just the same as you do, but if I can

---

[5] Gladys Bramley-Moore recounted that Miss Jean E. Cutler "was the governess at Russell Square for many years and became a good friend of all the children when they became adults. She often visited their homes and spent holidays with them." Laura, Dorothy and Gladys Bramley-Moore met Miss Cutler when they visited England and France to see their father's grave at Boulogne in 1931.

[6] Written on letterhead of The Royal Fusiliers, "The Sportsman's Battalion."

when we get over to Europe I will send you particulars. From all accounts the fighting is very fierce and it will take a lot of men to beat the Germans. We are getting on with our drill, and will soon be almost ready to go when called upon. I rather expect we shall leave some time in February, and that is early enough as it must be nasty in the winter, getting wet and then cold etc. Do you get my postcards I send? I have sent four or five at different times, and so far have not heard that you have got them.

I hope you will try to make yourself as pleasant as possible to your Mother & sisters. You are the oldest in the family and now that I am away, you must try to be a help, not a worry. This is a time of worry for a large number of people, and we should each remember when we grumble about some little annoyance that others have far more to put up with. We can't all have our own way, but we can all make up our mind to make the best of whatever happens. I want to see all my children enjoy life, and they can only do that if they determine to refuse to be annoyed by trifles. Trifles bother little people, not big ones.

A Happy New Year to all of you. You are seeing now the biggest war, I suppose, in the history of the world, and if Canadians have any right to be mixed up in it, it's a cinch that the Englishmen in Canada should be among the first to go.

With love to all
   from your affectionate Father
      A. Bramley-Moore

Thank your Mother for the Journal and Town Topics. I would have liked the Capital which mentioned my departure.[7]

---

[7] This refers to the *Edmonton Journal*; *Town Topics* was published in Edmonton under various names such as *Edmonton Town Topics* and *Weekly Town Topics*, between 1905 and c. 1919. Joseph W. Adair was its editor during the First World War. The *Edmonton Capital* was published in Edmonton from 1909 until c1914; its first editor and publisher was Arthur Balmer Watt, a friend of Bramley-Moore's; from 1910 until about 1914 William McAdams was the publisher.

10 England

LETTER 9

#179 [*Regimental number*]

Dec. 17th / 14
Hut 37
Sportsman's Battalion
Hornchurch

Dear Dorothy:
 Many thanks for [*your*] letter.
 You ask when am I going to the war. Well, I don't know, but I hope by the end of February anyway. Our officers tell us we may leave any moment, but I don't think we can go for a month yet.

Post card sent to Dorothy in December 1914, showing the Colonel and Adjutant of the Sportsman's Battalion at Hornchurch Camp.

 I am with your Granny for a day or two; they let me come to see if I could get any recruits.
 I have changed my platoon, and am now in "the thirteenth Platoon." The number of our battalion is the 23rd Service Battalion Royal Fusiliers (1st Sportsman's). They say 23 skidoo, but what with 23 and 13, which is supposed to be unlucky, we should have a hard time. I hope it doesn't mean we shan't get to the front which I would

think hard luck, because after all this preparation one would like to get there, and people are sure to say that one never really meant to get to the Front, "trust him to look after himself!!!" Perhaps you have heard that already. I can still smile if I get into the trenches.

The mistakes which we make in drilling sometimes are so funny. You see men wandering round like lost sheep, and trying to shelter themselves in a wrong squad so as the drill-sergeant won't see them!! But of course a squad which isn't theirs doesn't want them as it would upset them, so they "shoo" them away, and they go dashing round with a worried look till they land back where they ought to be.

Your Uncle Mostyn has joined the Australians; he is going to drive their motor lorries.[8] Your Uncle Leslie would like to join, but he can't pass the doctor because of bad varicose veins in his legs.[9] I had a small vein which the doctor noticed. Every two weeks or so the doctor comes round and looks at all our feet.

I saw Miss Hughes the other day and Miss Teetgen happened to be there. Miss Teetgen is matron of a hospital and hopes to go to Servia. She was Mrs. Lovely's sister.[10]

I try to write to you in turn but sometimes I forget whose turn is next and have to start afresh. You must all try to make yourselves useful, as girls have their part to play as well as boys. This war has upset everything, and you must determine that you will work at school, so that whatever happens you will be able to take care of yourself. Then you can hold your heads up; that is what our drill sergeants are always telling us.

With lots of love
    from your affectionate Father
        Alwyn

---

[8] Mostyn Bramley-Moore was a brother one year younger than Alwyn Bramley-Moore.
[9] Leslie Bramley-Moore was an older brother.
[10] Gladys Bramley-Moore feels that these references were to women who were "probably on the Bramley-Moore staff, maybe nursemaids or dressmakers."

12 *England*

LETTER 10

Grey Towers Barracks
Hornchurch
Jan. 2nd 1915

Dear Alfred:
Many thanks for moccasins which I received all right. Don't send any more as I think it is too wet here for them. It has rained all the time, and it makes me think of Danaker and his "Do you hear the rain a-falling, falling, etc." It must be horrid fighting in the wet.

This last week we have been digging trenches which form part of the defences of London, but that does not mean that we expect an invasion, but we have to be ready. We are getting on with our work and the Brigadier-General is highly pleased with us. I can't say when we will go. The quartermaster had just come in and said that two Zeppelins are coming this way but we can't see them yet.

The war looks as tho' it was going to last a long time. You children must all do the best you can to help your Mother and one another. Did you [like] those books I sent of London?

I daresay you have seen lots of pictures of trenches. My New Year's day was spent digging them. The big trouble is keeping them drained as it is cruel to be standing for hours in a foot or two of water.

I may put in an extract or two out of a newspaper. We have had no real cold weather - occasionally a little chilly.

Lots of love to all
    from your affectionate Father
        Alwyn

You might show the newspaper extracts to Joseph Adair.[11] You will find him at the Edmonton Printing & Publishing Co., Elizabeth Street, I think just east of Ramsey's. He is upstairs.

---

[11] Joseph W. Adair was a friend of Alwyn Bramley-Moore's. Born in Glasgow in 1877, where he learned the printing trade, Adair immigrated to Canada in 1899, where he worked on Toronto and Winnipeg newspapers. In 1906 he moved to Edmonton to work for the Edmonton *Bulletin*. In 1908 he took over *Town Topics*, and during 1915 published the *Western Weekly*. Between 1911 and 1946 he operated a linotyping business, and also served as an alderman on Edmonton City Council from 1921 until 1924.

LETTER 11

Jan. 19th / 15
Hut 37
Hornchurch Camp

Dear Dorothy:
Many thanks for [the] letters and papers. I did not get the chocolates, but I got the papers and letters from all of you. Don't send over the whole newspaper, but just cut out what you think I will be interested in. I wrote a letter to Town Topics the other day; your Uncle Leslie typed it for me and sent it off.

I hope the Govt. has paid by now. I wrote them a very strong letter, and I will also write to a friend of mine to look round and see if you are all right. If we have no friends, we must be very nasty people, eh? because nice people would have friends, and one should never mind receiving help from real friends; one doesn't like to receive it from enemies; we try to take by force from enemies but to receive with good grace from friends. What are friends for except to help when one needs them? I fancy I have helped some, and I don't mind being helped back. But I am afraid times are going to be bad, and you children must all get busy and work hard so as you can fight for yourselves.

Lots of love to all
from your affectionate Father.

LETTER 12

[LETTER TO THE WESTERN WEEKLY, 29 JANUARY 1915]

A. BRAMLEY-MOORE TO HIS FRIENDS AND THE WESTERN WEEKLY[12]

To the Editor, Western Weekly:
On New Year's Eve, I was at the point of dropping a line to you in order to wish all my friends in Edmonton and Alberta, a Happy

---

[12] The *Western Weekly*, "A Periodical of Independent Criticism on Matters Social and Political," was published in Edmonton by Joseph W. Adair and Sylvester Tredway for about six months beginning 22 January 1915.

and Prosperous New Year. Today I have just received a copy of your paper, and this time I intend to go through, and I ask you to convey personally to such mutual friends as you may meet, and through your columns, to other friends, my heartiest wishes for a Happy New Year. It may seem odd to read "Edmonton and Alberta," but it has a significance.

Your paper is at present confined to Edmonton, but it must in time increase its scope, and cover the whole field of Alberta. That is my New Year's wish for the new venture; that it may blossom forth into a real Albertan weekly. Your paper has avoided that snare, only too seductive in the West, of trying to run before it has learnt to walk. It has started from the ground up, and the laws of evolution clearly demand its expansion to a larger field; and I am certain that it would never be so unkind as to prove evolution wrong! That would be "the most unkindest cut of all."

By the time this letter reaches you, the municipal elections, of which I have just received word will have been forgotten; but I want to say one or two words to those engaged with yourself in the fight against monopoly in all its forms.

You cannot fight an organized enemy without proper organization on your own side. Individual bravery is helpless against organized cowardice, let alone against organized bravery, which is just as likely to be possessed by the enemy as by yourselves. "Capital" is always organized, if any serious attacks are being made against it. Pressure by banks, by the large advertisers, by the pulpit and the various societies which exist at the suffrance of capitalistic philanthropists, is always directed against the same enemy, "change." Reform represents change; change represents danger; danger unites the minions of Capital. Organization of a bunch of mediocrities will prove superior to the individual attacks of geniuses!!

You must subordinate self to the cause; you must cultivate an inward satisfaction at good work, without demanding public appreciation. Meredith has a beautiful passage bearing on this point, but I am unable to quote it from memory.[13] In the army, we are taught that the first and last lesson of the soldier is discipline. It is just as essential in the Army of Progress.

There is no special credit in doing good work if you receive payment in full, i.e., a sufficient amount of public applause. Credit is

---

[13] George Meredith (1828-1909) famous British Victorian novelist and poet.

due to those who continue to do good work although their pay may be hopelessly in arrears. That is what I want to impress upon the young people whose natural disposition inclines them to the army of change. Do your work unconcerned by the thought of payment. Aim at being a "superman"; and how can a "superman" be paid by a mere man? The foibles of smaller men whom you may have to humour, must amuse, not anger, you; the good opinions of your intimates must far outweigh any meretricious applause from the public.

Our late defeat must teach us lessons, not discourage us. In times like these, reaction is due to have its innings, and all we expect is that the imperishable fire of freedom shall be carefully cherished and fed, so that at the next favourable moment its effect may be more far reaching than ever.

One lesson, it seems to me, that has been brought home by recent events more than others, is the difficulty of successfully running a newspaper which may dare to speak out without fear or favour. It is a terrible thing from the point of view of public policy that newspapers should be "personal" organs, i.e., organs devoted to the interests of an individual. An organ devoted to a cause may develop narrowness; how much more, then, one devoted to an individual.

I am going to moot a possible solution. I do not expect that there is any chance that it could be adopted at present; but should fate deter me from again taking an active part in your public affairs, I should like to think that this idea may take root in the mind of some youthful enthusiast, and perhaps one day bring forth fruit.

A newspaper is hopelessly dependent upon advertisers. The bulk of the advertising, an amount necessary to the success of any paper, is controlled by four or five institutions. Any paper which ventures to pass beyond the limits of pious expressions of a desire to remedy the evils pertaining to our system of society, can be brought to time by the withdrawal of advertising patronage.

How can we remedy this? If the mountain won't come to Mahomet, Mahomet must go to the mountain.

In close alliance with our future newspaper, there must exist a departmental store. This store can be run on business lines, but it will constitute a weapon by which, if the newspaper is attacked, the war can be carried immediately into the enemy's camp. Successfully to be able to overthrow the enemy, we must be able to take the offensive; a departmental store permits of inroads into that bounteous land of retail profits; it gives us an offensive strength, the very presence of which may deter the enemy from attacking.

Difficulties; of course there are. But I start the New Year by believing that Alberta can produce just as good, and a little better, patriots than other countries have produced. And what man who has chosen to fight for progress, has been scared by difficulties? Teach your children Greek and Roman history. The examples of a Tiberius, a Caius, a Gracchus, a Demosthenes, and dozens of others, will surely stimulate your children to a degree of energy sufficient to surmount what difficulties there are.

In conclusion, let me protest against unwillingness to shoulder the task, because some grafters may manage to look after themselves. You are not going to abandon political or municipal government on that acount, are you? And you have been strong once in awhile, haven't you? Then why should you abandon a scheme which is full of possiblilities, and which may release journalism from those fetters imposed upon it by its dependence on commercialism?

Wishing you all, and the Camorra in particular, the best of luck,

Believe me, yours very sincerely,
A. BRAMLEY-MOORE.
23rd Service Battalion, Royal Fusiliers

LETTER 13

Feb. 1st/15
Hut 37
Hornchurch

Dear Alfred:

I think it is your turn for a letter. I have no news of special interest.

We keep drilling and digging trenches and sometimes get low spirited when we think that we are not getting on fast enough, and may still have to wait a long time before we get to the front. It is hard to say what will really happen, but I shall be disappointed if we don't leave by March 1st. I haven't heard much about the Canadians but the Princess Pats are at the front I believe.

If Mr. Hopkins sent me any cigars I have never got them; I was wondering if I would get any from Canada, so it is nice to know anyway that somebody thought of sending me some, and it is a shame I never got the chocolates the girls sent.[14] I wrote last week to Laura and sent off a lot of picture post cards.

I think drilling is making me hold myself up better and that is what you must try to do; not to stoop so much when you walk, don't look down on the ground. Keep your head up. Once you get into the habit of walking with round shoulders you will find it difficult to change, so stop it right now.

Alfred Bramley-Moore in his Boy Scout uniform, with Lassie.

You are at an age now when boys are difficult to handle, but you must remember that this period of war is not an ordinary condition of affairs, and that therefore you must try your best to correct your own faults. I remember I had a nasty temper when I was your age, and I often look back and wonder why the older people didn't pack me off somewhere by myself. Now you are the eldest of the family and should help your Mother to look after them while I am away, so do your best.

[14] Marsh Hopkins was a government surveyor who named several communities in Alberta; he wrote *Chance and Error: The Theory of Evolution* (London: K. Paul, Trench, Trubner and Company Ltd.; New York: E.P Dutton and Company, 1923).

You can't always do right, my boy, and you can't always be pleasant and nice instead of cross and ugly, but you can try and after awhile it will come easier. Of course other people must try to be agreeable too, but before we can blame other people we must look to ourselves. I feel sure you will grow out of your temper, and I wouldn't worry much about it if I was home and all was [the] same as usual, but as things are, if you can, why, make a big effort and hurry up and get past that stage of crankiness which boys seem to pass.

And that is why I want you to hold your head up; because I think that will help you to trust yourself if you are left to fight for yourself. Even if you are hard up, you can take up the law or medicine or engineering if you make up your mind that you will let no difficulties stop you. Read history; I wish you would read Greek and Roman history; and you will find some good stories in Smiles' works, "Self-help" and three others. They are red books and all in the den.[15]

This letter seems to be a lecture more than news, but I will send news when I have any, and you may feel sure that what I advise is not meant to stop any of your pleasures but only to add to them.

Lots of love to all from your affectionate Father.

LETTER 14

Grey Towers Barracks
Hornchurch
Hut No. 37
Feb. 16th / 15

Dear William:

I haven't had a letter from you for some time; have you got tired of writing? I am sorry to hear you have been ill again this winter; you must be sure to be careful not to get wet, and then in a year or

---

[15] Samuel Smiles (1812-1904), was the famous British journalist, biographer and philosopher of "self-help." *Self-Help* (1859) was his most popular and influential work; the "three others" mentioned by Bramley-Moore are probably the famous Smiles trilogy: *Character* (1871); *Thrift* (1875); and *Duty* (1880). These four volumes were given to Alwyn Bramley-Moore by his mother in January 1898, and are still owned by Miss Gladys Bramley-Moore. Smiles was energetic and hopeful, in contrast to other writers who took a more pessimistic view of the Industrial Revolution.

William Bramley-Moore.

so you will probably get good and strong again. I try to be as careful as I can, as I don't want to be laid up; but just now I am laid up with a strained ankle. This is the first time I have been ill since I have been here. Last week I joined in some hard runs before breakfast, and they must have been too much on the hard road for my foot, and so Monday morning when I started to run my foot gave way and I had to fall out and come back to my hut. I hope it gets well in a day or two; it is horrid limping round and not being able to trust to one's legs.

Have you played that game with the names of famous people much this winter?[16] I hope you have. You must learn to play with one another without squabbling. Did you finish reading "Before Adam" and did you like it? Whom do you like better, "Red Eye" or "Big Tooth"? I thought it was a nice story. I am sure you are working hard at your lessons, as I know you want to grow up to be a clever man.

I hear that the Canadians have gone to France to finish their training there, as they had so much wet and sickness at Salisbury Plain.[17] When I joined, I thought we would have been in France by now, but

[16] Alwyn invented a card game for his children. It included four suits, such as "famous women of history" and "famous kings." When any of the children lost, they were required to go to bed. Gladys, as the youngest, remembers that she quite often was the first sent to bed.

[17] Salisbury Plain is a barren rolling chalk plateau in Wiltshire, southern England, where most of the Canadian Expeditionary Force encamped and trained. The advance and billeting parties of the 1st Canadian Division crossed to France on 2 February 1915, and the entire Division was in France by 16 February 1915.

it will be some time yet before we go. Time goes very quickly. By the time this letter reaches you I shall have been a soldier about five months. I think you will find a change in my walking and in the way I carry my head.

    With lots of love to all
        from your affectionate Father
            Alwyn

LETTER 15

Grey Towers Barracks
Hornchurch
Hut No. 37
Feb. 21st / 15

My dear Dorothy:

Thanks for your letters. I am looking every mail for a copy of the Western Weekly, but it hasn't come yet. I got a letter from your Mother this week; thank her for it, and I will answer it next. I have so many of you to write to that it keeps me busy, while you only have one to write to.

They are getting a lot more strict now, and nobody wants to be punished now. The punishment is generally being "confined to barracks," or C.B. as we call it, or if the offence is very bad they are sent for seven days or more to the military prison at Warleigh barracks, where regular soldiers are stationed.

But when they are confined to barracks, they have to answer the bugle at the guardhouse every hour, and they don't like that. The bugler blows a tune of which the words are "You can be a defaulter as long as you like, so long as you answer your name." It sounds funny to us for the bugle to be saying that, but it isn't funny for the defaulter, I don't suppose. Most of the bugle calls have meanings in words. The call for the cookhouse says, "Come to cookhouse door, boys, come to the cookhouse door." The call for the guard says, "Come and do a picket, boys, come and do a guard; it isn't very easy, it isn't very hard." I don't know many others, but we all like the cookhouse call.

I have got a lame foot and can't walk without limping badly, so last week I acted as hut orderly twice so as to give my foot a rest.

I hope you are all working hard at your lessons. You will find it nice when you grow up to be able to read nice books, and be able to understand them; and you must learn to be able to understand your own language as well as foreign languages; and one should at least know one's own language. Do you give one another dictation; and do you read stories out loud?

Now I must close, as cookhouse has just sounded and dinner will be here in a second, and first ready, first served. The men are hollering out "Cook house orderly, come hurry up, let's have our grub once a week," I'm not orderly today.

Lots of love from
   your affectionate Father
      Alwyn

LETTER 16

[*Written on Sportsman's Battalion letterhead*]

Grey Towers Barracks
Hornchurch
Hut No. 37
Feb. 25th/15

Dear Alfred:

I hear that you are doing well at your work. I am very pleased to hear it.

I have been laid up more or less with a bad foot these last ten days, so I haven't been having a very strenuous time. It is an awful bore not being able to walk without limping. I do hope it will get well soon. I have been holding it under a water tap for half an hour at a time, but it seems very slow in getting well.

Last Sunday we had a parade to hear the findings of a court martial read out. We were drawn up on three sides of a square facing the Grey Towers; and then the prisoner, a corporal, was brought out into the centre between two guards. The colonel and adjutant appeared on the scene, and the adjutant read the sentence which was that Corporal Smith was reduced to the ranks for being drunk. Then the prisoner was marched away and the Colonel made an inspection of us. As a rule they cut off the stripes when the sentence is read, but they didn't do that [*this time*]. I saw the prisoner in town in the afternoon and he looked very happy and apparently is quite content to be a private.

They are getting stricter all the time with us, and I wouldn't want to be caught laughing in the ranks by our present captain; he is a regular tartar and wants us to toe the mark now. I hear that that is the usual custom in the army; to break the men in gently!!

I don't know when we will be moving; we hear lots of rumours and now I have given up listening to any of them. I think the war will last for another year or more anyway, so that one need not get worried that he won't get a chance to do all the fighting that is good for him. We are certainly getting drilled enough.

Stick to your work lad, and make yourself pleasant to those at home.

With lots of love
from your affectionate Father

LETTER 17

Grey Towers Barracks
Hornchurch
Hut No. 37
March 2nd / 15

My dear William:

How are you getting along? Are you quite well again? You must remember to take care of yourself as you don't want to be always sick, do you?

We are drilling away and digging trenches. We are tired of digging trenches as we don't think they will ever be needed, as the Germans are not likely to be able to land in England.

They are getting a lot stricter with us now, and I am pretty careful not to be caught laughing in the ranks by our new captain. We go out sometimes and have sham fights, one company against another. Our captain thinks he is very clever, and one time he got us all behind a bush, and when he saw the enemy coming on, laughed and said, "Ha, Ha, We've got them; I'm sorry for No. 3 Company," and took us out to attack them. But we all thought the opposite, and that No. 3 Company would have wiped all of us out, as we had let them cross the open country without firing at them at all, and then, when we came out, they were close to us, and could shoot us as we came into the open. On one or two other days we figured we would all have been killed owing to the tactics of our clever captain. Once the adjutant (he is next to the two colonels) popped his head over a wall and said to our captain, with a wave of his hand, "You are absolutely annihilated, absolutely." Our captain didn't like it, but we all thought it rather funny. Of course in real fighting when the bullets are flying, the bullet will let one know whether one can advance or not, so that our clever captain may soon learn that he hasn't always got the other fellow.

I don't know when we will be leaving here; we are all getting tired and will be glad to go. I have been in the army five months now, so I ought soon to be ready to go; they always said it would take six months, tho' I thought it would have taken less.

Lots of love to all and hoping you are working hard,
    from your affectionate Father
        Alwyn

LETTER 18

Grey Towers Barracks
Hornchurch
Hut No. 37
March 9th / 15

My dear Dorothy:

Please thank the children for all the valentines they sent. They were very nice. I have just written to Laura. I got the ones Gladys and William sent. I am sorry William isn't keeping up first place, but perhaps he is just resting himself a little and intends to dash on again when the warm weather comes. 8 and 10 is not so very bad in a class of 36.

I have very little news. My foot seems better and I hope will give no more trouble. We hear rumours that we will be leaving here soon, but we have heard that so often that we don't pay much attention to what we hear. Tomorrow a general is going to inspect our drilling; today one was going to look at our huts but he didn't turn up. I was orderly today and we gave everything a wonderful cleanup.

The grass has been green here all winter. It is no longer so muddy, which makes it pleasanter. I have been away a long time, eh, but I

Three girls reading together.

am no longer my own master now. Once you are in, if they want you they can keep you.

You must all learn to help one another, as that will make it easier for all. I am so disappointed if you children haven't been playing that game of names we made, because you used to like it. Nothing more of interest today.

So with lots of love to all
from your affectionate Father
Alwyn

Tell Laura I don't think I am clever enough to make a valentine, and anyway the time is long past now. Dear me, who would want me for a valentine!!

LETTER 19

Grey Towers Barracks
Hornchurch
Hut No. 37
March 21st/15

Dear Alfred:
    I am glad to hear that you are doing well at school.
    Here we are still; fussing away as I call it. Yesterday I was made a Lance-Corporal (so now you can address your letters to Lce. Corporal Bramley-Moore). I am rather pleased as I never asked for promotion or tried to get it as I didn't really want it, as a non-com [*Non-commissioned Officer*] has a lot of work to do I don't like. He has to know (or when he gets a little higher) by heart a lot of rigamaroles about what you do in sloping, presenting arms etc. and of course he should do it smart himself. An officer has far easier work than a non-com; in fact an officer's job is very easy, but too much standing round to suit me; they stand shivering when it's cold looking on while we anyway have a chance to keep warm.

We have been doing skirmishing work lately, and also are starting to practice night attacks as most of the attacks take place at night at the front. We have no idea when we may move; sometimes we hear that we are a rotten battalion, and again we hear that we are a fine battalion. I should rather like to have a little fight in Turkey first before going to Germany, as it would [*help*] to have the two different experiences.

I am quite a soldier; have learnt to be quite tidy, fold my clothes up at night, clean my boots, sometimes my buttons, and of course we have to fix our beds properly when we get up. We are just like boys at school with a man's knowledge. We have to keep our tempers! because if we use abusive language to any superior we could get into serious trouble.

Lots of love to all, and thank Dorothy for her letter, just received, which I will answer soon.

From your affectionate Father

LETTER 20

March 28th / 15
Hut 36

Dear Dorothy:
We changed huts the other day, and 36 is the new number. We all moved over into this hut except four, so we are still the same crowd. I have never got the Western Weekly with my letter [*printed in it*]. Do you read many books; you should read some of the stories aloud I used to read to you, Blue Bird or Aksenoff, but I suppose you are now filled up with stupid Jewish stories, instead of stories written by men who loved their own mind better than ghosts.[18] People have

---

[18] *The Blue Bird: A Fairy Play* (1909), was written by Maurice Maeterlinck (1862-1949), the Belgian poet and dramatist who won the Nobel Prize for Literature in 1911. A.T. de Mattos' English translation of *L'oiseau bleu* (1909) was very popular internationally. This optimistic allegory suggests a transcendence of death. Ivan Dmitrich Aksenov was the protagonist of a short "folk tale" written by Leo Tolstoy in 1872. In "God Sees the Truth, But Waits," Aksenoff is falsely accused of a murder and sent to Siberia where he spends the rest of his life. Although he lives devoutly in prison, and even forgives the man who caused his imprisonment, he dies in prison. Reference to "stupid Jewish stories" suggests Alwyn's generally critical approach to the "Judeo-Christian" tradition of the various Christian denominations, and to the Bible in particular.

believed in hundreds of different kinds of gods or ghosts, but none of them are real. The christians call their special ghost "the god of love," and yet see how different christians hate one another, so that the Methodists have different tea parties to the Presbyterians and so on. The Romans had lots of gods or ghosts but they never quarrelled over them, as they soon came to know that each god was only an idea and represented something, and was not really a person who interfered. Thus they had a god of war, a god of wisdom, a god of love and ever so many, and they were always polite to the gods of their enemies.

You should try and read history; I suppose you think this is silly but I think people who can only think of dresses and hats are silly!! Perhaps we are all silly. We had a field day on Friday and a General came to look on. Three companies were to attack the other two. The half-company I was in was the reserve force, and we never got near the enemy, so we had a very easy time. I hear that the General was very displeased with some of the officers because everything had been badly arranged. The defenders had taken up such a strong position that the attackers had no chance, and he thought that was stupid. He wanted them to fight, not to sit where they could not be attacked.

I can't understand why you haven't got the Govt. money; every time I write they say orders have been sent to pay.

Love to all from your affectionate Father

Alwyn

LETTER 21

Grey Towers Barracks
Hornchurch
Hut No. 36
April 3rd 1915

Dear William:

I got your letter and found only one mistake. But some of the work I call a little untidy; it is not much use being right if people can't tell what figures you mean.[19]

---

[19] William sent a long-division exercise to his father with a short note written in a large hand: "Will you correct this long division? I am not tired of writing ... letters. From your loving Son William Bramley-Moore." His father marked it and returned it with this letter.

We don't sing much now, as we generally have our band with us when we are out. It plays "Rule Britannia" and "Tipperary."

I am surprised to hear that you liked "Red Eyes" best; why, he was supposed to be the villain of the story!! Still it is better to be a Red Eyes than a crying weakling who can't stick up for himself, but I thought "Big Tooth" (I think that was his name) was very nice and no coward.

I enclose Laura's sum corrected as I have just written to her. Dorothy's letter has just come; thank her for it.

Our work is more interesting now, and we go rushing about field and over hedges, one company attacking another one, and we also go out at nights. I think I told the girls in one of my letters how we hold on to one another's coat tails. I do hope we move away soon as it is getting a little tiresome being here so long. Almost six months; in fact in 5 days it is six months since I joined. I didn't think a soldier had so much to learn. We have to lie down flat and then get up, run forward twenty yards and lie down again in four seconds. With a rifle and a bundle on one's back it takes some doing. When we have all our equipment on you would think we were horses with harness on. We have ever so many straps; all together it makes a good bulgy load.

I am glad that you are getting perfect in your work, as the more you know the better you will be able to look after yourself when you grow up. A country prepares itself for war, and children prepare themselves for getting their share of the good things in life, and the more you prepare, the more you may get if you are good stuff.

Lots of love to all
    from your Father, Alwyn

LETTER 22

Grey Towers Barracks
Hornchurch
Hut No. 36
April 11th/ 15

Dear Alfred:
    I have just got your letter and five others; they all came together although the postmarks differed on some of them by two or three days. I am glad to hear that you are going to sleep in the tent again

"Granny." Ella Bradshaw Bramley-Moore, with Rev. William Bramley-Moore, at 26 Russell Square.

and I think it does you good. I suppose you will spend some of your summer holidays at Heathcotes.[20] How is Reggie getting on?[21] And has he told many tall yarns about his trip to Cold Lake?

I can't tell how soon we will get out; I had thought we were bound to get out [in] under six months, but now I wonder if we will be out in the next two months. They have so many thousands waiting to go and they can't all go at once. The General inspected our Company, carrying on a sham fight the other day, and he said he was very pleased indeed. He probably said what he meant as the last time he was down he gave some of the officers a great wigging.

I was reading to your Granny the last time I was in London,

---

[20] The Heathcote family lived near the Bramley-Moore homestead in the Kitscoty district, just west of Lloydminster. Elijah Heathcote managed the Battle River Collieries coal mine of which Bramley-Moore was vice-president at this time.

[21] Reggie Kirkpatrick was a school friend of Alfred Bramley-Moore's.

Tennyson's poem about the "Revenge."[22] Sir Richard Grenville with this one small ship fought 53 big Spanish ones, and destroyed four or more of them, and only ceased fighting when he had no ammunition or powder left. You will find the story in a volume of Froude, "Short Studies in Great Subjects," under the heading "England's Forgotten Worthies."[23] It is on the bookshelves, look it up and read it. He is the type of man we are descended from, and we must show that we have some of the same stuff in us. On your mother's side you have Scotch in you, and they are great fighters; they have enlisted for this war better than the other races; there are a lot of them with us in this battalion.

I am glad you are getting on with your studies. Make the best of your time.

Lots of love to all
from your affectionate Father
Alwyn

LETTER 23

April 29th / 15
26 Russell Sq.

Dear Dorothy:
I have had no news from any of you for a long time, but that may be because the Second Canadian force is supposed to be on the way over, and most of the boats are used to carry them.[24]

---

[22] Alfred, Lord, Tennyson (1809-1892) wrote his epic tribute to Sir Richard Grenville in 1878; Grenville was anchored at Flores, in the Azores, aboard *The Revenge*, when attacked by a Spanish fleet during the reign of Queen Elizabeth I.

[23] James Anthony Froude (1818-1894), was a popular English historian who wrote a history of England in twelve volumes. He is now best known as literary executor and biographer of Thomas Carlyle.

[24] The first units of the 2nd Canadian Division embarked from Halifax, Nova Scotia, on 18 April 1915. Colonel G.W.L. Nicholson wrote in his official history of the Canadian Expeditionary Force, that "shipping was so difficult to secure that the Department (of Militia) was forced to request the Admiralty to divert sufficient transports to carry the remainder of the contingent." These finally arrived in England during May and June, several months behind schedule.

I am going back to camp today. I have had a long holiday through being quarantined on account of Clifford.[25]

I enclose a drawing done by Ruth;[26] she seemed to run it off in a minute or two, but then her Mother was a good drawer and taught them all when very young how to draw. Ruth was very anxious to see me salute an officer, and used to look out of the window to see if one was coming, and wanted me to dash out so as to pass him when I would salute. But as none came I took her out for a walk, but we had to go a long way before we met any, and then we met quite a few, and I solemnly gave the salutes.

I am in a hurry as I am just going to report to the Military Doctor that there have been no fresh cases of scarlet fever, and he will send me back to camp.

Lots of love to all

from your affectionate Father

Alwyn

Ruth Harris' sketch "Putting on Swank"

[25] Clifford Harris was the son of Alwyn's sister, Millicent. He was born 24 October 1904 at Christ's Hospital, near Horsham, Sussex, and was the youngest of three children of Rev. George Harris, school master there. His mother was the cousin of a famous medical missionary, Dr. Theodore Pennell, whose ministry was to the North-West Frontier of India. During February 1916, Clifford Harris was stricken with cerebro-spinal meningitis, called "spotted fever" then, and sent to St. Bartholomew's Hospital in London. On 2 February, Harris rallied, and on 17 March was sent back to Horsham to convalesce. Bramley-Moore appears to have been exposed to his young cousin's illness and quarantined as a result. On 22 October, Harris went to King's College to read theology. He later spent years in Iran for the Christian Missionary Society, and died there on 4 March 1930. His story is recorded in R.W. Howard, *A Merry Mountaineer: The Story of Clifford Harris of Persia* (London: Christian Missionary Society, 1931).

[26] Ruth Harris was about one year older than her brother Clifford; her mother, Aunt Milly, was an artist who had etchings accepted at the Royal Academy.

LETTER 24

May 3rd / 15
Hut 36
Grey Towers

Dear William:

I have just read your letter to Granny. She was very pleased with it. I have been quarantined here (26 Russell Sq.) but go back today. I heard that they were going out this morning to camp out for three days, so I dashed off on an early train so as to be in time to join them; when I got there I found they were not going till the next day, so, as my pass was good till the night, I hurried back again to 26, as I may find it hard to get leave again as I have been away 17 days this trip.

Corporal Bramley-Moore sporting his new moustache.

I hope you liked the photos. Thank Laura for the Western Weeklies, which I enjoyed. I suppose you will be commencing to think that I am never going out, but there is no hurry as the war isn't nearly over yet.

From what I can hear the soldiers consider it a great piece of luck to get wounded in the leg or arm, as they all figure they must get wounded somewhere. But if you only get a very slight wound, they hurry you right back to the front, so a wound has to be just so to let one still be able to get about but not fit for fighting; but the Germans haven't got time enough to choose any special place to hit, so one just takes his luck. We are all anxious to get over to try our luck.

32   *England*

You will hardly know me with my moustache; I think it looks very grand and I will leave it on till I come back. One of my chums always calls it a "scrubbing brush!!" but it is getting better all the time.

I am always glad to know where any of you are in your classes so long as you are not at the bottom of the class. I suppose that was where Dorothy was, as she wouldn't tell me.

Lots of love to all, and hoping that nobody ever hears any whining or crying from anybody in the house.

From your affectionate Father
        Alwyn

LETTER 25

Grey Towers Barracks
Hornchurch
Hut No.36
May 11th/15

Dear Alfred:

I am sending off a [*photograph of a*] group of three of us to you. I will send some to the others in a day or so. W.P. Black is the one in the middle, and A. Millen the one on the side. Black has been in the States and at Hamilton, Ont.; he is a Scotchman of Irish parentage. He was going to fight with the Ulstermen against Home Rule and he trained there with the Ulster Volunteers. Millen is a Kentish farmer. Kent is the county South and East of London. The three of us used to have tea together at Romford almost every Sunday afternoon in the winter, so we had this photo taken and gave the lady of the tea shop one.

We had a General inspect our Company some time ago. He stopped and fussed about this and that strap, and kept on saying that there was nothing like uniformity. I call him Old Uniformity. Black was standing next [*to*] me and the General turned him round to look at his pack and explain just how he wanted the straps and the water bottle etc. to hang. When a man is standing to attention he hasn't any support and a little shove will always knock you over, so the General almost shoved Black over; he apologized to Black. I had great difficulty to prevent myself from roaring with laughter as I saw Black grinning a bit. I would have got

Alwyn Bramley-Moore, W.P. Black and A. Millen, Royal Fusiliers.

into a row as the Colonel, Captain, Adjutant and all were just in front of us.

I don't know how I will like the gas, but I daresay it is not any worse than being close to a "Jack Johnson" when one drops.[27] The

[27] The Allies nick-named the German 5.9 and 8 inch shells "Jack Johnsons," a tribute to the world heavyweight boxing champion. John Arthur Johnson (1878-1946) was the first black world champion, and held the title from 1908 until 1915. These shells also were sometimes called "coal boxes" because they created black smoke when exploded, in contrast to the Allied shells which used lyddite and sent up yellow smoke.

34 *England*

Canadians had a hot time.[28] No news about our going out. I hear that we belong to the Third Army. We are getting drilled into machine soldiers all right. We were out for three days the other week.
    Lots of love
        from your affectionate Father
            Alwyn BM

LETTER 26

Grey Towers Barracks
Hornchurch
Hut No. 36
May 16th / 15

Dear Dorothy:
    Many thanks for [*your*] letters. Did the buttons get over all right, and were they what you expected?
    We have had a fairly quiet week, but next week I believe we are going to march twenty miles a day on three days, so that will keep us out of mischief. Twenty miles with our pack on our backs makes a good day's march. The packs are not at all comfortable and are heavy enough.
    We frequently now have very easy days; sometimes we lie down on the grass and send semaphore signals to one another; of course, we have to stand up to send the signals but we lie down to read them. Then again we spread out and lie down, and a man goes off and tries to hide from our sight while still being able to fire at us, and we have to see how quickly we can locate him; they call that "visual training." Then the section commander has to learn how to describe the spot he wants us to shoot at so that we can all pick it up instantly. You see frequently you have to shoot at a spot where nobody can be seen, but where you think some enemy are concealed. If it is nice and warm, it is quite pleasant doing this work. Sometimes I go out and do the hiding. We also shake a rattle which

---

[28] Between 22 April and 4 May 1915, the 1st Canadian Division suffered high casualties in the Ypres Salient. There during the Second Battle of Ypres the Germans first used chlorine gas against the Allies.

imitates a Maxim [*machine*] gun, and you try to detect where the sound came from.

I told William I got his chocolate. I will send you and W [*William*] and G [*Gladys*] photos of the three of us and you may like them. I sent your Mother some of my postcards for my album. I wonder if I will get many picture postcards in Europe this time.

Lots of love to all
    from your affectionate Father
        Alwyn

LETTER 27

Grey Towers Barracks
Hornchurch
Hut No. 36
May 22nd / 15

Dear William:

I am running very short of news as our days here are all much the same; only the weather gets hotter and that makes us grunt carrying our heavy packs. We are all longing to move; we hear that in a fortnight we are going to Yorkshire to do our brigade training; that means there will be four or more battalions camped together and they will practice all together. You see you first start with squad-drill that is about 8 men together; then platoon drill which is about 50 or 60 men together; then company drill which is 4 platoons together; then battalion drill which is 4 companies together, and then brigade or divisional drill which is four or more battalions drilling together; so then after that we are ready to go to the front, so if we go to Yorkshire we will be at the last

William Bramley-Moore.

36   *England*

lap. I fancy they have found out that it is useless sending troops not properly trained to the front, because no war has ever been so hard on the nerves, and good discipline is essential. Next week we are going for an 80 mile march, but we will take four days, though twenty miles a day carrying your pack and a blanket is enough.

I often think of Cold Lake and wish I was up there with my two boys, as when I come back you will be big enough to come if you are not behindhand in your studies. I am enclosing an article from the Daily Mail which I thought might interest Alfred, and then he might pass it on to Bernard Gee if he is still at the club, and he can give it to Adair.[29]

Lots of love from your affectionate Father
   Alwyn

LETTER 28

Grey Tower Barracks
Hornchurch
Hut No. 36
June 1st/15

Dear Alfred:
   Thanks for [*the*] letter. I hope you succeed in passing well. I suppose when the holidays come you will run down and visit Mr. Heathcote and Ashworth.[30] It is a splendid thing to get away from the city occasionally and stay right in the country as there are things one learns in the country and not in town and vice versa.
   We are having some long marches this week with our packs on; walking on these hard stone roads is very hard on one's feet, and a good many fell out with sore feet; I stood it pretty well, but was quite pleased that we couldn't go today as a General came to inspect us.
   We expect to move from here now any day, and we shall all be glad. When we move we will probably go to another place in

---

[29] The Gee family were Barr Colonists; Bernard Gee later moved to Edmonton; "the club" probably refers to the Edmonton Club.

[30] The Ashworth family were neighbours at the Kitscoty homestead. Gladys Bramley-Moore recalls that her brother William "spent his summer holidays at their farm. Their youngest son was about William's age. I believe he later owned a garage in Marwayne."

England for a few weeks where we can drill with other battalions. I shall be glad to get away as I am getting tired of this.

The march to Berlin doesn't seem any easier than the march to London by the Germans, but perhaps if all the world helps we may be able to beat them. Minnie was surely right when she told you that the German army was wonderful. So far this year they have got the best of it as they seem to have licked the Russians badly. It looks like being a long war.

I hope you read good books occasionally and especially history; this war should make you interested in the history of all the various countries engaged. I like Marlborough best of English generals.[31]

With lots of love to all
    from your affectionate Father
        Alwyn

LETTER 29

Grey Towers Barracks
Hornchurch
Hut No. 36
June 6th / 15

Dear Dorothy:

I was glad to hear that you and Laura were nearly top of your classes.[32] Perhaps I will be able to pay you some time, but if not you must seize some books or something, I suppose.

Are any roses out yet; a lot of roses are out here already. Your holidays will have started by the time this letter reaches you; I hope you will all try to make one another's holidays as pleasant as possible.

Next week we are going for three long marches. Luckily my foot has never bothered me since I had it attended to at London. I was talking to Miss Hughes the other day; she looks very well. I suppose the babies of Mrs. Hopkins are getting quite large.

I am very tanned, but keep very well. I should like to get out soon, as I am getting very tired of staying here so long, though I

---

[31] John Churchill, 1st Duke of Marlborough (1650-1722).
[32] All the Bramley-Moore children attended McKay Avenue School, and later attended Victoria High School. This old red brick building was overcrowded when Gladys attended, so she took grades 9 and 10 in the Armouries, an annex to Victoria High School.

Alwyn Bramley-Moore's mother and father at 26 Russell Square.

have been very lucky as this camp is close to London and I often run up to 26 Russell Square. Your Auntie Lucy is staying there just now. The trains are filled with soldiers.

I have just heard that Major Anderson is a prisoner; I used to see him at the club and liked him.[33] Would you like me to be a prisoner? I would take care not to quarrel if I was, tho' it is hard to keep one's temper in the hot weather; once or twice I have felt like telling a superior officer to go where it is still hotter, and then there would have been a row.

With lots of love

from your affectionate Father

Alwyn

[33] Lt. Col. Peter Anderson DSO, was born in Denmark in 1868, and was brought to Canada by his family in 1880, arriving in Edmonton in 1891. Working as a brick and stone mason, he was able to establish his own brick business in 1899. This soon became one of the major Edmonton businesses during its building boom, but was destroyed in the great flood of 1915 while Anderson was overseas with the Canadian Expeditionary Force. Anderson joined the 101st Regiment, Edmonton Fusiliers, in 1908, and served with them as the redesignated 9th Battalion, CEF. Captured in April 1915, while serving with the 3rd Battalion, he was made a Prisoner of War at Bischofswerda, near Dresden. Anderson became an Alberta celebrity at this time, and recounted his experiences in *I That's Me: Escape from German Prison Camp and Other Adventures* (Edmonton: Bradburn Printers Ltd, c.1920).

LETTER 30

Grey Towers Barracks
Hornchurch
Hut No. 36
June 16th / 15

Dear William:

Sometime since I heard from you, but I suppose you find it hard to write in the long summer days. I hope you are growing and getting strong and fit. In which room do you sleep? And who are your chums now? If you like fighting other boys, you had better take some lessons in boxing, but I hope you won't fight boys smaller than yourself.

I am trying to transfer into the Princess Pat's [*Princess Patricia's Canadian Light Infantry*], but it seems as if I shan't be able to as the War Office doesn't like anybody over here joining the Canadians. I was at the Canadian camp at Shorncliffe on Saturday; they are very comfortable there and have a nice place.[34] We are all getting very tired of staying here, but I suppose all the soldiers can't be fighting at the same time.

I haven't heard whether the girls got the buttons all right. Next winter when the nights are long you must read some history. I would like to have your photographs; we can get them done very cheaply here; mine only cost four cents apiece. Uncle Alfred will be over here in a few days; I suppose he is joining the Army Medical Corps. Is Mr. Johnson acting as stretcherbearer? We get up at 5:30 in the morning now. Some Zeppelins came very close to our camp the other day. They expect a lot to come over sometime.

What do you think about war? Tolstoi, the Russian who wrote the story of Aksenoff, thought war very stupid; do you remember

---

[34] Colonel G.W.L. Nicholson wrote: "Before the 2nd Division left Canada, Ottawa expressed to the War Office its concern that there should not be a repetition of the unfortunate conditions encountered by the First Contingent at Salisbury Plain. The selection of Shorncliffe Camp, near Folkestone, was warmly welcomed, and early in March the Militia Department offered to furnish all tentage required by the Second Contingent."

the story of Ivan the Fool who wouldn't fight when his country was invaded?³⁵ Hoping all are well.

    With lots of love
        from your affectionate Father
            A. Bramley-Moore

LETTER 31

June 30th/15
Hut 4
23rd Royal Fusiliers, E Company
Hornchurch

My dear Alfred:

    I have been a little slack in writing lately, but I have been so bothered and annoyed. I am trying to change into the Princess Pats and there are ever so many difficulties which keep cropping up. I don't know if I will succeed or not. I have left my Company and am now in E Company where all the men are who are waiting for commissions or transfers. I hate it. All my chums are gone, as the other companies have gone north to Nottingham: so you see I am in a new hut. I am so sorry about Mr. Johnson; it seems far worse when it is a person you know well. Major Watts had dinner with us at Russell Square today.

    Lots of love to all from your affectionate Father
        Alwyn

LETTER 32

Grey Towers Barracks
Hornchurch
Hut No. 3
July 3rd / 15

Dear Dorothy:

    Many thanks for [your] letters. I am glad to hear how well you are getting on at school. Who are your special friends now? We are having a nice summer and the country looks very pretty. I hope

---

³⁵ Leo Tolstoy published "The Tale of Ivan the Fool" in 1885.

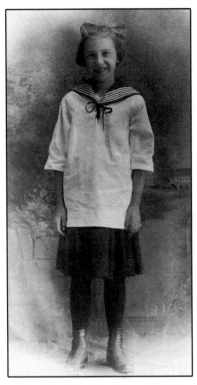

Dorothy Bramley-Moore 1915.

you will manage to have your photos taken, as I should like to see them.

You will be grown up young ladies when I get back; I hope you will grow up sensible and friendly and not always be turning up your noses like some modern young ladies do!!

I expect in the next letter you will get a new address and hut number as I hear we are going to move to a camp about 2 miles away, where a few are left the same as here, and then that will leave one camp entirely empty for new troops.

I don't think I will see Cold Lake this year; I would so like to be up there now; the ducks will be pleased to know that I am going to find out how funny it is being shot at!! If I ever get over, as it seems awfully slow in getting there, but I guess the war will last long enough to give everybody a chance.

It is my birthday today; so far I haven't had any kisses or kicks; not even a pat on the back. I saw your Uncles Alfred and Swinfen the other day; both looked well. I saw Colonel Jamieson of Strathcona[36] and Major Watts in London last week. We have two prisoners in the cells. One has to stay there seven days, the other for 28 days. We keep a man outside their cells night and day.

What books have you read lately? I thought you were going to write a story and send it to me.

I hope you get a pleasant holiday; you musn't leave Alberta for good as it is good to grow up with a fine new country like it is.

With lots of love to all
    from your affectionate Father
        Alwyn Bramley-Moore

---

[36] Lt. Col. Frederick C. Jamieson, Officer Commanding the 19th Alberta Dragoons, which went into action on 11 February 1915.

LETTER 33

Hut 3
Hornchurch
July 10th / 15

Dear William:

I hope you are enjoying your holidays. I am trying to make a move here, but it seems almost impossible to get anything done. I am anxious to join the Canadians as the pay is better, and times are so bad, but one can never get answers; a letter is written and then gets lost, and week after week passes and nothing is done. If brains are going to win the war, then I think the Germans will win as I can't see any heavy brainwork on our side, except perhaps in the Navy. Luckily, our men are born fighters, so they are hard to beat even with no brains to help them. Of course I can only see a little, so I may happen to see a bad part and it may be all right in other places; but we drill and drill away at movements which (a lot of them) will never be used at the front and the men who are waiting to become officers spend their time peeling potatoes and doing other chores instead of learning things useful for an officer. They have to be taught something later, but why should two or three months be wasted peeling potatoes!!

I am trying today to see Bennett, who is over here with Borden, as if he chooses he may be able to help me, but so far I can't get into touch with him.[37]

I don't like it with all my chums away. Your Granny sent me a birthday cake but I sent it on to my old section. Thank Dorothy for the chocolate wrapped up in Town Topics. I generally move my bed outside the hut now and sleep in the open; I like it far better.

---

[37] The Rt. Hon. Robert Borden, Prime Minister of Canada, wrote in his Memoirs (1938): "I spent the week-end of July 10th-11th with Sir George Perley at Sunningdale and had a long conference with him as to the status of High Commissioner." Perley had sent a cable to Borden on 1 June 1914, "expressing Bonar Law's desire that I should visit England that summer." Andrew Bonar Law was Colonial Secretary in the Asquith cabinet during 1915-1916. The Rt. Hon. R.B. Bennett, Prime Minister of Canada from 1930 to 1935, was Conservative Member of Parliament for Calgary East at this time. Bennett accompanied Borden on his wartime trip to England.

I have seen ever so many people about the Government money; they will pay from Oct. 8th all right; apparently some papers were lost.

Lots of love to all
from your affectionate Father
Alwyn

LETTER 34

Grey Towers Barracks
Hornchurch
Hut No. 3
July 17th/15

Dear Alfred:

I was glad to hear from you and hope that you will have passed handsomely in your exams. Your Mother tells me you will be going to Mr. Heathcote's for a while. When you are there give my best wishes to Mr. Heathcote, Fos and his wife. Tell them I am getting rather tired of soldiering over here.

They seem to think that if you can carry your rifle at the correct slope that they have made you into a good soldier. I have heard people laugh about the Germans and their goose step, but a lot of the things they do here are just as funny. I have been trying hard to get into the Canadians, but they won't give me permission so far. I might ask for a commission but I am rather afraid I might be put into a regiment which would be staying here for another six months, and I would like to have a look at the front. There was a lot of talk about the desperate things we were going to do this spring, but now summer is passing and we have certainly not done much.

I hope you will grow up to be a good Albertan; Alberta is a big enough country to be proud of and you children have grown up with it and should look upon it as your land. I was born here, so this country has claims on me but if I pay those claims then you won't owe them.

What are you thinking of doing when you grow up? You must soon be making up your mind so as to study for that purpose. Read your history, don't forget Shakespeare and good books. I always liked history.

I am afraid I won't see you this year. Be sure to call on Ashworth and all my friends, and give them my best wishes and tell them I am still a philosopher. I think the nations will go into bankruptcy after this war; we will all have to start afresh and [on] a fair field more or less to everyone.

With lots of love
> from your affectionate Father

LETTER 35

July 25th / 15
Hut 24, 23rd R.F.
Gidea Park, Essex

Dear Dorothy:

I am glad you have all done so well at your exams and I hope you will have a good rest and go for a change somewhere. You mustn't despise the country as you can get lots of fun on a farm.

That story about Major Anderson's legs being cut off is a lie from what I hear. Nobody here knows anything about it. And prisoners are not allowed to put any stamps on their letters, so he couldn't have written underneath one. You mustn't believe all the wicked stories you hear. Germans and Austrians are just the same as we are, some kind, some cruel; none of the Germans you knew were cruel. And of the two boys George and Billy who worked on our farm; George was an Austrian and he was a nice boy. Billy was almost as much Russian as Austrian, and though sulky perhaps, he was nice enough. I enclose a copy of a German soldier's letter printed in an English newspaper; it doesn't seem very savage.

I have a wretched time now and hope soon for a change. They seem to treat us more as criminals [than] as volunteers; they bother you about such stupid things.

I hope you will play plenty of indoor games together when winter comes; there are enough of you to make things very pleasant if you all try to be cheerful to one another. We must learn to make ourselves happy. No more news just now so -

with lots of love to all
> from your affectionate Father

"German Soldier's Letter"
[*undated newspaper clipping enclosed in letter*]

The "Vossische Zeitung" quotes an interesting letter from a soldier to his little sister, who had written to him asking him "to kill a lot of Russians" and "to gain a new victory in order to cheer us up." He writes:

"Kill a lot of Russians." You have not seen them lying about - these poor men with their singularly solemn faces. You have not seen the battle which preceded, and the bad wounds which so many of my friends got in trying to kill all of them. You do not think of the fact that those dead men had parents, brothers and sisters, whom they loved. And you have not seen the harrowing destruction of the villages and towns - how the ... hunted-down population is running away leaving everything they had behind to be consumed by the flames.... But then, remember we are not fighting in order to cheer you up, we are not ... starved and suffering from wounds and home-sickness in order that you at home may be cheerful at the tea or beer table. We are fighting and bearing this terrible wretchedness in order that you may be spared the horrors of war, and that [*the*] future may be bright."

LETTER 36

Hare Hall
Hornchurch
Hut No. 24
[*30 July 1915*]

Dear William:

I got the newpapers with the stories of the floods in [*them*]; they must have been exciting. Did you see much of them? Thank Dorothy for the papers. I am sorry you are having poor weather; on the whole we are having splendid weather.[38]

> [38] The flood of 1915 destroyed much of the residential and commercial development in the North Saskatchewan River valley. Gladys Bramley-Moore recalls that "a Children's Shelter was in a red brick building in the Flats and canoes were used to rescue the children and take them to safety. I remember my Mother taking me to a place where we could see the river, probably 104th Street at McKay Avenue School, to watch the canoes going to various buildings."

I am in a new camp but I hope not to stay here long. I am still trying to join the Pats. I was down there last week but the first papers I sent were lost, and we have had to send fresh papers. There are rumours that the Sportsmen may be going soon, so if I don't get into the Pats I shall try probably to get back to my old platoon. I am thoroughly sick of drill here; we are supposed to be very smart, and it's "Look to your front," "Keep stride," "Stop talking" all the time; and then there are one or two pups of officers, but I daresay on the whole we are lucky. Most of the stuff they teach us is of no use at all in actual warfare. At Clystone tho', where I should have gone if I hadn't been trying for this transfer, they have been practicing attacking trenches and throwing bombs. Nowadays bomb-throwing seems to be the chief form of attack. I wrote to Bennett but he wouldn't answer my letter.

I shall be glad to hear that you are getting on with your lessons, and that you have had a good holidays. I suppose you are getting big and strong now; you must make yourself as useful as possible and laugh oftener than cry. I am often "jollied" about my smile, so I am still alive!! I can't help smiling to think of having to put up with the insolence and ignorance of a lot of dubs instead of enjoying the freedom of Cold Lake. How I long for it.

Lots of love to all
    from your affectionate Father
        Alwyn

LETTER 37

Savoy Hotel
London
August 8th/15

Dear Alfred:

Here I am still kicking my heels in Essex, so I really have very little news. I hope you pass all right. We have just heard of the loss of Warsaw; that Russian steam roller one heard so much about seems going the wrong way. I hope you had a jolly time in the country and got a few prairie chickens. I would like to be with you, as I am getting tired over here. They should have told us at the start that we were no good to them unless our backs were perfectly straight and our noses just so... because it is difficult to get the correct "dressing" if noses and stomachs are different sizes. A lot of us are too old to be suddenly changed, and we think it a lot of rot; I am sure there are lots of foolish Russians and Turks who are doing good fighting and could not keep a very straight line. Where I am now they expect men to stand to attention when speaking to a corporal!! We didn't always do it at Hornchurch when we were speaking to officers. I find as a rule that the less they know of actual military life the more they fuss over trifles; I don't see how a big man could condescend to be so trivial as they are. However it makes us more philosophic as it makes us sick of the whole job. I have come so far that I want to get to the front, otherwise they could all go to blazes for all I care, and Cold Lake would see me again, but no chance just yet, I am afraid.

Writing in a hurry; I am leaving my dinner waiting to see Bennett and guess I will have to go without seeing him after all. Just as I wrote that Bennett walked in. I have had quite a chat with him and he thinks if I can tell him exactly where the papers are that he can get my transfer arranged. He has been terribly busy he tells me and couldn't possibly see me before, so I must apologize to him as I was certainly getting very cross at finding it so hard to see him....[39]

From your affectionate Father

LETTER 38

Hare Hall
Gidea Park
Hut No. 35
[*No date*]

Dear Dorothy:

You see by the hut number that I keep changing huts but I haven't moved yet. I ought to know soon. The Captain calls this the "casualty hut" because he puts in it people he expects to leave soon, and

[39] On 8 August 1915, Borden met Lord Bryce regarding future constitutional relations within the Empire. Max Aiken and Bennett were with him as he visited Bristol and received the Freedom of the City on 9 August, and toured military hospitals there. Bennett had early associated himself with the P.P.C.L.I., and his brother, George, enlisted with the first draft of that regiment. He was therefore in a position to exercise his influence to facilitate a transfer to the PPCLI. It was also at about this time that Bennett heard that George Bennett had contracted enteritis in Flanders, and was hospitalized.

others who are on odd jobs.... There are only about four of us who sleep in this hut; but a few others eat here.

I have very little news because one day is just like the next; we just have the evenings and the weekends to look forward to; I have been fairly lucky in getting passes, so I quite often see your Granny and Aunt Lucy. Aunt Lucy was very busy for a while making drugs for the Govt. but they worked so hard and quick that they soon made far more than was needed. She was very disappointed at stopping work as she liked it.

Corporal Alwyn Bramley-Moore, Royal Fusiliers.

We get drilled more and more, and far more savagely than we used to be; somebody or other is all the time saying, "If I catch you moving I will put you in the guard-room," "If I catch you laughing, I will put you in the guard-room," and so on all the time. I call them rotters and pups etc. but not to their faces!! just yet. You are only supposed to put a soldier in the guard-room for a very serious offence, but these ignorant bullies are always threatening it and often do it. They would sooner lose the war and have you drill smartly than win it and have you drill poorly. I think the Germans must have let loose a drill microbe which has eaten up the common sense microbe, because you rarely see common sense here.

Lots of love to all
    from your affectionate Father
        Alwyn

LETTER 39

(Hare Hall
Gidea Park)
Hut No. 35
August 25th/15

Dear Alfred:

I have just got news from the girls that you have passed; I am pleased to hear it and hope you will enjoy your new school.

I am expecting to hear that I am transferred to the Canadians any day now as now that Mr. Bennett of Calgary has been trying to have it put through, I think I will succeed. I don't think anybody yet has succeeded in getting a transfer, so I will have reason to feel pleased if I succeed. I think you had better write to Russell Square until I am fixed more definitely. At present I am back at Hornchurch, only for a few days, I hope, looking after the camp until another battalion comes and takes it over. I think they will come very soon, as a Colonel came and looked over it today, and said he would come directly he got permission from the War Office.

I hope you have been swimming this summer; you ought to stick to it till you can swim easily. I suppose you will be back home by the time this letter reaches you. What sort of crops [are] at Kitscoty, and whom all did you see? I wonder how my canoes are at Cold Lake.[40] I sent a photo of myself to Preshoff but never heard if he received it. You will stick to your work and must soon be thinking of what you intend to be as your studies should be dictated by your intentions somewhat. I have just got a photo of Dorothy; it is not first class; she seems to have grown.

It will be a long time yet before I am back unless I get badly wounded as the war doesn't look like finishing yet awhile. There was no hurry after all to get to the front as we will all have a chance and it will be better when one knows one's own side has as big and as many guns as the other side.

Lots of love to all
    from your affectionate Father
        Alwyn

[40] The canoes were left at Cold Lake when Alwyn heard that war had been declared in August 1914. He returned to Edmonton immediately to leave for England to enlist. The canoes remained at Cold Lake for years.

The Bramley-Moores on their homestead at Kitscoty, Alberta.

II. WITH THE PRINCESS PATRICIA'S CANADIAN LIGHT INFANTRY

LETTER 40

Sept. 7th 1915
Pte. Bramley-Moore, No. 1834
No. 4 Coy: P.P.C.L.I., 11th Res Bn
St. Martin's Plains, Kent, Shorncliffe

My dear William:
    I think it is your turn for a letter. Perhaps some of mine went down in the *Hesperian*, so you must make allowance for a gap.[41] I was sworn in as a Princess Pat today and am now stationed here with them.[42] I haven't had time yet to find out whether I shall like it better, but I hope I shall. There are only a few fit men here and they may send another draft over any day, so I may be gone almost by the time you get this letter. I wish to go as I am tired of hanging around here and it won't be so pleasant here as at Romford, as I shan't be able to run up to London so often.
    It is a beautiful place here; I went this afternoon and had a swim in the Channel. I was able to go as my name had not yet been published in orders as having joined and I am still wearing my Fusilier uniform and badge. I will send the badge to Laura as she lost hers. The uniform must be given back to them. I was a free man more or less for a week. Now I am a prisoner again. The doctors examined me very carefully and kept fingering my varicose vein but it never bothers me.
    I think your Mother will get $35 this way, as they take $15 from my pay and add it to the $20. If there is a gap between payments, the Patriotic Fund should be made use of. There was one week between for which no pay was being paid to me; but I am wondering how quickly they can notify Ottawa to stop paying allowance.
    Lots of love to all
        from your affectionate Father

[41] The Allan Line ship *Hesperian* was torpedoed and sunk 85 miles off Fastnet on 4 September 1915, with the loss of 32 lives.
[42] Alwyn signed his Attestation Paper on 6 September, 1915, transferring from the 11th Reserve Battalion to the P.P.C.L.I. He enlisted with the Patricias at Shorncliffe on 7 September, 1915.

Regimental badge brooches such as these sent home by Alwyn Bramley-Moore were popular souvenirs of the war.

LETTER 41

September 14th/15
P.P.C.L.I.
80th Brigade, 27th Division
B.E.F.[43]

Dear Alfred:

I am here with the Pats waiting to go to France at a moment's notice, so you can write to the above address, which will be my new one. Only [the] usual number of stamps. A draft has been made of 15 of us and we are waiting to go at a moment's notice. We first thought we were to have gone today but now it looks as though we will be a few days longer.

It is pleasant enough here as so far I have done no drill. Today we did a little firing in the miniature range and go for a route march this afternoon. We are not allowed out of barracks which is rather tiresome when the date of departure is uncertain. Six went absent last night and have to go before the A.C.[44]

I shall be glad to set my foot on French soil. We go first to Rouen. They have made me a Lance Corporal again. I don't think these men could drill like the men I left but you don't make use of the drill at the front. They send lots of these fellows over pretty soon after joining, and I thought at first that they wouldn't take me

---

[43] British Expeditionary Force. The P.P.C.L.I. joined the 80th Brigade on its formation at Winchester in November 1914, and remained with the B.E.F. until November 1915. The Regiment marched to billets at Pradelles on this date.

[44] Possibly Army Council.

because I hadn't completed my musketry course, but they have overlooked it as I said I was anxious to go.

I am glad you passed and hope you will get on well at the [Victoria] High School. While I am away you must help the younger ones. I think it is far better for the older men to fight than for youngsters; some of us older ones have had our share of life and the young ones are only starting their lives, and if I don't come back you must be willing to help the others till they get on their feet; you will all soon be grown up and able to look after yourselves, and a few years at the start of helping one another won't spoil your lives. Always try to be cheerful and be friends with your brothers and sisters. Real friends don't get angry with their friends' shortcomings but bear with them and try to stop them from doing what they might be sorry for afterward.

Lots of love to all
    from your affectionate
    Father
    Alwyn Bramley-Moore

LETTER 42

Sept. 18th/15
P.P.C.L.I.
80th Brigade, 27th Division, B.E.F.

My dearest Laura:

You can write to the new address now as by the time you get this I ought to have got to the trenches. I can't tell you what company or platoon I shall be in as I won't know till I join the regiment. I am quite pleased at having got over before the Sportsmen as I got fooled for such a long time [*and was*] sure they would be out first.

I have nothing very wonderful to tell you yet. I have arrived at our regiment's base and don't know when we will move further. I enjoyed the journey so far and they were a very nice bunch of fellows. I think I shall be very proud of the Pats.

I had charge of a prisoner on the way, but he was quite willing to come along and we all thought that when we got here they would remit the balance of his sentence, but to our disgust they didn't. If you commit a "crime" here, of course you expect to be punished, but you don't expect to be punished here for a "crime" which occurred in England; the actual leaving for the firing line should set one free. I was very annoyed as I had cheered him up on the way by telling him they were sure to let him off.

I daresay your letters may not be as frequent now as they were when I was in England but you needn't worry about it, as I may be quite all right and yet unable to write.

Lots of love to all
    from your affectionate Father

I hope you play games together now that the nights are getting longer and that you don't need me to keep the peace! If children who are brothers and sisters scrap, we must expect different nations to scrap.

LETTER 43

Sept. 19th/1915
P.P.C.L.I.

My dear Dorothy:

I haven't had any letters for some time but I daresay I will get a number at once. Letters will be very welcome in the trenches, so write often and cut out interesting things in the paper. Not about the war as we see English papers, but about politics etc.

I haven't been long waiting since I joined the Pats, have I? We are waiting quietly for a day or two at the base before we go forward.[45] All quite peaceful here and magnificent weather; one would almost believe that the war is only a horrible dream as there is such little difference really between the various white races, but apparently they take it very seriously and are determined to blow one another up. I can't help smiling at the trouble they take about it, tho' it's no joke, as they kill the young instead of the old. It wouldn't matter so much, would it, if the old people chose to kill one another, but the old people stay behind and send the young ones to fight because the old ones managed affairs so badly that all the fighting is necessary.

---

[45] The Patricias marched to Hazebrouck on 18 September 1915, where they entrained for Guillancourt the next day. They then marched to Mericourt-sur-Somme, where they bivouacked in a field just outside the village, and where this letter was likely written.

I must write and tell [*Joseph*] Adair that if youngsters of 18 are good enough to fight and be killed they should be good enough to vote. The old fogies won't like that, because when we are young we are full of enthusiasms and generous thoughts, not all the time of course, but at times, so the young try to make things right, while the old say it's no use trying because they can't be made right. I daresay they can't, but I like to see the hopeful youngster who tries and I hope all my children will have each a good spell of youthful optimism before their blood gets chilled and soured as years pass by.

Be true to your friends and don't sneak. You can be pretty sure that you are living right if you find that people like and welcome you; because if living wrong makes you liked and welcomed why then living wrong perhaps is living right!! Make the best of things; you are not the only pebbles on the beach and have no more right than any other person to have things made easy.

I shall hope to see you again but if I don't you must make the best of things, help one another and smile instead of cry.

Lots of love to all from your loving Father.

LETTER 44

SEPT 27TH/ 15
P.P.C.L.I.

My dearest Dorothy:

I am just getting ready to leave this camp and move on to the front.[46] I would never have got there if the war had been as short as a lot of people expected, but I felt sure it would be a long war.

I think I would sooner be shooting ducks with Alfred up north, but I always thought when I was shooting ducks that it would be only fair to be shot at oneself, because the duck didn't have much chance to protect itself. So now when I come back I shall be able to tell the ducks that I took a chance of being shot! Perhaps they won't care anyway; especially if they think I am a poor shot.

Girls grow into young women very quickly so you will soon be brought into contact with life's problems. You will find a lot of

---

[46] The Regiment marched to their hutments at Froissy, on the Somme, on 20 September, 1916. Five days later they went into support trenches at Cappy, while No. 4 Company went into Brigade reserve at Eclusier, where this letter probably was written.

pleasant and a lot of unpleasant things, but don't create unpleasant things for yourself; we must have both as the unpleasant helps to make the pleasant pleasanter, so put up with it and it will soon pass away. You may have to help yourself, but lots of others have to also, and all should; if you stick to your studies, you should be able to hold your own. But always remember to help your brothers and sisters, and when you learn a useful thing, be anxious to teach it to them. Don't always want to be away playing, but help your Mother in the house and play games without quarrelling. Play your best and don't get angry if you don't win. I shall expect to come back and find you all very clever and very happy.

Our happiness depends upon ourselves chiefly, and I hope all my chicks will learn how to get their share of it. I dislike the churches and would sooner you learnt how to conduct yourself; I don't think you will ever take it too seriously anyway. One's life is really a comedy, but we often treat it as a tragedy; it never really is, as it's all so trivial in comparison to all lives put together.

Lots of love, dearest Dorothy
    from you loving Father

LETTER 45

Sept. 27th/ 15
P.P.C.L.I.

My dearest Laura:

It is a long time since I have had any news, but I expect to find a lot of mail waiting for me when I reach my regiment. We are starting in a few hours.

It is just about exactly a year since I left Edmonton; I shall be quite a stranger when I come back. Who occupies my chair at the table? And to whom does the den belong? I'll bet some of those poor books wonder if they are ever going to be opened again; how sad they must feel now that they have no companion to sit up with them till 3 or 4 in the morning. No tea in bed for a long time, and no little girls or boys to annoy by giving them dictation when they want to go out or play.

You are my eldest girl and must act as your Mother's helper with the rest of the family. I don't think house work is so terrible if all pitch in and do their share without an hour's grumbling and fussing first on the grounds that he or she did so and so yesterday and the other should do it!! I have learnt in the army that the quickest and best way is to do things promptly and then you get spare time, but if you put off things [*you*] are never done.

I hope you will keep on studying and aim to make yourself independent. There are many paths open to women nowaday. I shall always hope that one of my daughters take up medicine, and becomes a swell with their own motor like Emma Webster.

We must give and take in this world; there are so many other people beside ourselves and it makes an awful muddle if everybody is trying to go in a different direction; but don't be a sheep either, and be always following without knowing where you are going. Have your own goal to aim at, but if you can reach there by a roundabout way and travel with others that's all right. It will please the others, and there's generally lots of time. I hope my girls will always be close chums and also chums with their brothers.

Lots of love, dearest Laura, from your loving Father

LETTER 46

Sept. 27th/ 15
P.P.C.L.I.

My dear William:

I sent you a military post card the other day; did you get it? We are leaving this base camp this afternoon and going to join our regiment at the front, so by the time you get this letter I will have heard all the noises of battle and seen some of the sights. I will write when I get chances but don't expect letters regularly.

There are a lot of things I would like to tell you but I will hope that you will learn most of them for yourself. Stick to your work and your friends. Don't be frightened of aiming high, but don't betray or forsake friends for the sake of place or money. Always remember that there are two sides to every case and that the other fellow may be right; it would be a funny thing if we were always right when we know that other people are not always right. Give a helping hand when you can and don't sell friendship; if you give a friend something you musn't think he should give you something back; if he does, then you have given him nothing; you have only traded. I don't want to bore you with advice as you are a child yet, but you may remember one or two little things. Always look after your health [and] don't abuse it; if you have health and friends you must be leading a pretty sensible life. You know I have no use for the churches; you will judge for yourself when you grow up but don't let others judge for you. Read good books and don't be always playing. I wish I could read "The Blue Bird" to you again. There, my boy, I shall hope I shall come back, but if you make a man of yourself I shall have left something behind to take my place.

Lots of love, my dear little boy
   from your loving Father

LETTER 47

Sept. 27th/ 15
P.P.C.L.I.
80th Brigade, 27th Division, B.E.F.

My dear Alfred:

We are just leaving the base for the front so I shall soon have news for you about the actual fighting line. I have heard a lot of stories but they all seem different, so one must see for oneself.[47]

You won't mind me giving you a few tips, will you, as I may not get the chance again? If I don't come back, you will be more or less left in charge of your younger brothers and sisters; that will mean that you must help them, and when they make mistakes must try to put them right. Children may quarrel among themselves, but the one in charge must not quarrel with them, so you won't do that. They will soon all be grown up, so it won't take much of a slice out of your life looking after them.

Over here they are always clamouring that the youngsters should go and get killed and leave their fathers comfortably at home, but I think that is a rotten view. You are too young at present anyway, but if you were older, it would be proper that I should go first, not you.

[47] When the Regiment moved to permanently occupy a section of trench, it was very close to the German lines. Agar Adamson, Second-in-Command, wrote to his wife that "It promises to be very uncomfortable. Hardly any light will be possible at night and a very alert watch will have to be kept. The whole Regiment with the exception of a company, will always be in the trenches and 6 machine guns; unless we go forward before, our tour will be one month. The place is full of great big rats who can polish off a pair of boots in a night."

But you must be ready to take my place for a while and get the younger ones started; I know you will try. We older men have more or less had our innings and have not got so much to lose, and we want our children to take our places and then we shall live. I don't believe in any life after this one, but all you children are part of me so that I am still alive in a sense.

You will soon have to make up your mind what you are going to be; if you mean to be good one, it pays to put up with some discomforts and stick to the schools and take law or medicine; but other callings are just as honourable; farming is all right if you like it, but no profession is any good if you are ashamed of it. You are inclined to be easy, but make up your mind that you are going to be as good as the best.

Stick to Alberta and be an Albertan and then it won't be your business whether Servia or Bulgaria becomes larger.

Lots of love, my dear boy
from your loving Father

LETTER 48

To a child of 9; Edmonton, Alberta
Oct. 1st / 15
Platoon 16 No 4 Coy, PPCLI
80th Brigade, 27th Division, B.E.F.

My dear William:

I sent you one of the official postcards the other day, but I think it is your turn for a letter as I won't count the six I sent at the same time.

We are in sound of the guns now all the time; sometimes we hear big booms, sometimes the rattle of the Maxims and occasionally rifle fire. At present we are not at the storm centre but there is heavy fighting some distance away on both our flanks.[48]

---

[48] The Regiment went into the front line at Frise on this day. Major Stanley L. Jones wrote to his wife on 1 October that the regiment was "taking up this part of the line tonight for probably a month unless we move the Huns before then, which let us all hope. We would sooner do a long spell like this and have a longer rest afterwards. You will see we are not in the heavy fighting here but if our people succeed farther up, this part of the line must also advance."

We live in barns now; this country seems full of barns and they all seem in as bad a shape as the barns were on the White farm in Ontario.[49] And the rats!! As soon as we put the lights out they start and run round and round the walls close to our heads, squeaking and generally making themselves objectionable. I don't like them but it makes me laugh to think that I don't like them. I think I would sooner have children crawling over me than rats; we used to have dozens of them in our barns in Ontario, but I think they were better fed there, while here they have to rustle.

We came in box-cars from the base; so you see I am in 16 Platoon No. 4 Company; my section is Number 13, so I don't get away from that number. My old regiment expects to be at the front about now, but I haven't heard for sure yet. The French soldiers get 2 cents a day so they think we are well paid; there are a good many of them round here, and a nice smart appearing lot they seem. This village was occupied by the Germans, and a lot of the buildings have been destroyed by gun-fire. It reminds one of a deserted tumble-down Indian village, only larger.

I suppose you have been back at school for a long time; I hope you are keeping near the top of your class. Who are your chums now? Don't be too rowdy in your play and never pick on the weak; I would sooner you fought bigger than smaller boys, but I don't think much of fighting. Never sneak. You must read "The Blue Bird" aloud to Gladys.

Lots of love to all and to my dear "big" boy
   from your loving Father

LETTER 49

Oct. 3rd / 15
Somewhere in trenches

My dear Alfred:
You are the first to be written to from the trenches. We came in yesterday evening and were on sentry go all night; now we are partially resting for the day in the dugout and the rear trenches, and

---

[49] After their marriage, Alwyn and Nellie Bramley-Moore lived on a farm near Sombra, close to Sarnia, Ontario. They farmed there from 1899 until 1903.

return to full duty at night.⁵⁰ Very cold night for this time of the year, followed by a magnificent day; very much like the weather we would experience up north, shiver[ing] in our bed clothes at night and back in the sun during the day. Do you remember how Teddy [*Frederick Balmer Watt*] used to be wrapped up in the fur rug? and the nightly solemnity of your grand bed-making?

I am sitting at a table on a cut-out earth seat writing this.⁵¹ I got a slight snooze this morning, but my eyes seem to think they would like more. I can imagine day after day at this job must get fearfully monotonous, and if the weather or trenches are really bad it must be too miserable for words, but for the first time it is interesting enough.

Not that you see much except a ridge which we suppose is the enemy's trench, and countless barbed wire entanglements. Then in the morning you see smoke arising from the trenches, and you may toss over a shot or two just to prevent them from stretching their legs! There is a continual desultory rifle fire, and now and again guns. Some dust fell on me from the concussion of a shell I shall say. Just like a few raindrops.

Two of our officers got wounded this morning; Cowley and De Balinhard ; the latter was the officer of my platoon and although I didn't have time to know much of him I am sorry to lose him and like the way he shaped; he is wounded the worse of the two, but I think both will recover. They got it from the same shrapnel shell, and another officer was with them but didn't get hit.⁵² I find it still

---

⁵⁰ Agar Adamson wrote that the men during this tour "only got 6 hours sleep in 24 and we insist upon them lying down the moment the rest hour comes. They are up all night and all stand too from 6-7 p.m. and 5-6 a.m." Adamson felt that No. 4 Company, in which Bramley-Moore served, was in "a most dangerous part of the line. The right of (its) trench garrisoned by one Platoon is in a trench at the top of a quite high hill. The German trench is only 15 yards away and they are constantly bombing and hand grenading each other." The War Diary for this date notes that there was "quite a lot of sniping and a number of whizz bangs were fired into the trench occupied by no. 4 company. Lt. DeBallinhard and Lt. Cowley were wounded."

⁵¹ Stanley Jones wrote on 2 October that there were "lots of quite comfortable spots in the old houses as long as the shells don't reach them, and the men have plenty of dugouts with stoves and all kinds of furniture, just as the French troops had them last winter."

⁵² Stanley Jones reported that during the night "my men saw the Germans pulling the body of the man I shot back into the trench, so we are about square so far, as (Charles) Stewart's men killed three this morning."

difficult to realize that I am in any more danger than say at Cold Lake; in fact I know the knowledge of a loaded gun somebody is holding in the same rig or canoe would keep me more alarmed, but of course I have had no taste of a terrific bombardment. I can imagine that shakes one up. At night time you look over as you like but not in the day.

I will tell you more in other letters. I must leave something to say. I owe Gladys a letter. I won't forget.

Lots of love to all
    from your affectionate Father

LETTER 50

Oct. 5th / 15
P.P.C.L.I.

My dear Gladys:

I am writing this sitting on the ground in a large barn, but tonight we have three fires going and I have fetched in some straw to lie on, so I expect to sleep sound, as I have been two nights in the trenches and come back apiece to rest. We call the place we come to "billets." I don't know how long we shall stay here; as a rule, I think, two days in the trenches and two days out; but of course changes are often made.

I got letters from all of you which were brought to me in the trenches and I was glad to get them. I got the paper in which it mentioned how much you had collected; very clever of you I think.

This life reminds me of the way we managed when we came from Saskatoon to Lloydminster; we might be a bunch of freighters, only we have rifles instead of horses to look after.[53] The guard-room I have just been in looked for all the world like an Arab's shack or any Indian shack.

The second night in the trenches a German came right over to our wire entanglements and took a shot at me or somebody else; I shot back but didn't hit him; it was dark of course and I could only shoot into the spot where I had seen the flash of his rifle. The sentry

---

[53] Gladys Bramley-Moore notes that her parents spent time in Saskatoon after they moved west from Ontario. They met the Barr Colonists in Saskatoon and later moved to Lloydminster with this group, travelling in wagons, and sharing the privations of that infamous trek.

thought he heard him at our wires, but we didn't really believe a man was there; next time we must be quicker.

We stay awake all night in the trenches and take turns at resting in the day. There is a lot of shooting always going on, but not many hits. The casualties occur in the big offensives, but at present we are not where a big offensive is taking place.

Almost a year since I enlisted. How do you like it without me to bother you? I'll bet Laura and Dorothy are glad they get no dictation. Give my very best love to everybody and keep a lot for yourself.

With best wishes
    from your affectionate Father

LETTER 51

Oct 11th/ 15
P.P.C.L.I.

My dear Laura:

I am sorry you are so particular about not writing except in answer to a letter; you see you have one to write to, and I have six of you to write to, not counting your Granny and various Uncles and Aunts of yours, who are all pleased to get a letter from the front and have all been very kind to me. Don't get into the habit of imagining that you should only give to the same extent as you have been given; that spirit kills all real friendship; one gives to one's friends in proportion as one is able; not in proportion to what the friend has given us; it is the same with visits; we don't bother with friends as to whether they owe us the next visit; we go when we can; perhaps it is easier for us to go than for them to come; with acquaintances who are not friends we may say, "Oh well they owe me a visit," but not with friends. Trading presents or visits is not giving, and we don't trade with friends; just the same way, my dear girl, you will bear with a friend's failings where you wouldn't with a stranger's, for you cannot be a friend, a real friend, to a person if you get cross immediately you discover they are not little Jesus Christs. You won't mind a little advice, will you, as you will soon be a young woman and I want you to be broadminded and not fall into the petty ways of little people.

There is one soldier here who wrote a letter to a paper or society as a lonely soldier, and he got some answers. So for a joke some of the other fellows wrote him a letter and signed it from Lulu Walker, Billinsgate. In the letter "she" said how she admired the heroic soldier etc., and how she would be proud to do a little to soften his hardships, and made it appear she meant to send a parcel. The soldier (whom we will call X) was ever so pleased, and saw in his mind's eye a good big parcel coming, but as he told his mate, "the stupid old fool forgot to put her full address; she just put Billinsgate." The others told him he might chance it, that that address might find her. So the other day when I was putting my letter into the pile, I saw sure enough a letter addressed to Lulu Walker, Billinsgate!!! Now Billinsgate is the name of a famous meat market in London, and there is probably a Billinsgate P.O. Well, I said to myself, this joke might be given another turn. I wrote at once to Uncle Les and told him, and asked him to get somebody to ask at Billinsgate for Lulu's letter, and then send X a parcel; and I told him to write to X and say that Lulu knew of course that such a heroic man like X couldn't enjoy anything without sharing with his section, so that she sent the parcel to the section!! It will be a joke if the parcel comes; I don't know yet if Uncle Les will do it or not; they may not like asking for the letter, but as there is no Lulu Walker, I don't see any harm and I hope they carry it through, and then those who wrote the letter will be surprised, as I haven't told them. They will think that by chance there was a real Lulu Walker at Billinsgate!

You can send me an indelible pencil and any little thing any of you care to send will be welcome. Yesterday I had a great old wash in a brook, for I have to wash all my clothes now myself. We can only have what we can carry with us. That is like the Indian lives; only he may pack a canoe or a pony instead of his back. I can't always remember what I have said in other letters, so you must excuse if I sometimes repeat myself.

Make yourself perfect in spelling, and reading. Have you had no dictation since I left? Give my love to my books, poor dears; I suppose nobody loves them now that I am away.

Lots of love to all from your affectionate Father

A. B-M.

LETTER 52

Oct. 13th/ 15
Trenches
P.P.C.L.I.

My dear Dorothy:

I am just scribbling you a line in a dugout about 50 yds from the Germans. I got a letter from you in the trenches; we always like to get letters. We have a great old time cooking in these dugouts; we make our fires in old pails in which we knock holes and we make our tea, fry our bacon, sometimes make a stew or frenchfry potatoes! So we don't starve. We drink a lot of tea, but I like cocoa for a change.

Yesterday morning the Germans sent over about thirty bombs from their trench mortars; they tear up the dirt where they hit, but you can easily see them coming through the air. It's lucky you can see them, as if they hit you full you can't see yourself!! There was nothing left of one fellow but his boots, but he didn't belong to our regiment. We had three casualties tho' from one of them, and our trenches knocked about in pieces, but they are easily fixed up. We replied to them with our big guns; I don't know how many miles behind they are but they are some distance, and they have to hit a place just about 30 or 60 yds from our trenches, so they have to shoot straight. They call them "whizz-bangs"; you can't see them but, you can hear them whizz through the air.[54] There is a lot of rifle shooting at night, but not many killed, if any, just once in a while. But you have to shoot in order to make them good! As if you didn't they would look over the trenches as they liked. It doesn't do to show your head for long! I think I told you or Laura of the Germans I saw the other day.

This is about 2 p.m.; I have just had a nice sleep and a wash, as I go on duty again this afternoon and night. I am quite happy, but hope I shall be back to see how clever you all have grown. But please don't put me in the corner just yet! Perhaps I'd better bring my gun back with me!

Lots of love, dear Daughter, from your affectionate Father
A. B-M.

---

[54] Allied troops called the small, low-trajectory, 3-inch German shell common along the Front a "whizz-bang." This was due to its sound: a distinctive "whizz" when it was fired, followed by a bang when it landed.

LETTER 53

Oct. 19 / 15
P.P.C.L.I.

*"The Dog and the Shadow." A Tuck's Post Card popular during the war.
"A dog, carrying a piece of meat in his mouth, saw the reflection of it
in the water; and snatching at the shadow lost the meat itself....
Germany has lost the prosperity she had so labouriously acquired,
in the vain endeavour to obtain the mastery of the world."*

My dear William:

I was very glad to get your letter in the trenches. I have just had a long letter from Laura; thank her for it; I think it better to write in turn than keep guessing whom I shall write next to, and if one of you misses a letter you may be pretty sure it got lost in the mail. I daresay there was a letter on the *Hesperian* or *Arabic*.[55]

I was pleased to hear that your class voted you to be the best reader; that shows our time wasn't wasted in reading Aesop's fables. I wonder if I shall be back in time to have Gladys read to me.

When we were in the trenches we were only about 35 yards from the German trenches. I used to see them at times. I got a shot at one

---

[55] The White Star Line ship, *Arabic,* was torpedoed and sunk off southern Ireland on 19 August 1915; the *Hesperian* met the same fate on 4 September 1915.

once, and he waved back a shirt to show I had missed, but it must have been close or he wouldn't have known it was for him. For the last two or three days in those trenches the Germans sent over a lot of trench mortars at us; you can see them coming; they turn over and over in the air like a big jam pot and then there is a second or two passes after they hit the ground, followed by a great explosion. I was acting sentry in a bay and saw them well; the closest fell about 10 yards away; they often caused the dirt to fall over me; wouldn't want a dozen to be playing at the same time. We had [censored] casualties in our Company in two days; [censored].[56]

We are now at a rest camp so-called for two weeks, and after that we will probably go to different trenches; I hope they are nice dry ones like the ones we were in. It is very miserable at this camp [*Morcourt*]; we are not allowed to move about further than 500 yds. and we have to do a lot of stupid drill which is no use for fighting, but might look pretty when some of the heroes who keep away from trenches come round in their fine clothes. I don't think the French are fooled about the same as we are, but of course they are not paid near as much, and they know they are fighting for their country. "Present arms" won't save France, but England and Canada are not in the enemies' possession, so they have time to play at soldiers, and it does please some of the dudes!! but not the soldiers.

I hope you will stick to your work; I want you to be a big swell when you grow up, but with your brains, not with your money.

Lots of love to all
    from your affectionate Father
        Alwyn

LETTER 54

Oct. 29th/ 15
P.P.C.L.I.
L/C Bramley-Moore, P.P.C.L.I. 1834

My dear Alfred:

Very glad to get your letter with the news. I haven't been in the trenches for some time and have therefore no special news of

[56] The P.P.C.L.I. were relieved by the Cambridgeshire Regiment and were withdrawn to reserve at Morcourt on 16 October 1916.

Alwyn and Nellie Bramley-Moore on the Sombra farm in Ontario, ca. 1900.

interest. We have been marching a bit and changing quarters and are wondering where we will find ourselves next.[57] I have no idea myself but perhaps I musn't tell you even what some of us think. There are always rumours, and it is like betting on a horse race when you bet on any special rumour; you may pick the winner, but it's perfectly certain you didn't know when you picked him. But I don't think they will leave us idle for long, as with the new campaign started in the Balkans, they won't have any spare troops for a while.[58]

I am glad that you are reading Muhlbach's works as they will teach you a lot of history.[59] When you get interested in one of them, look up the history of the wars of those times and see how it compares

---

[57] On 24 October 1916, the Regiment marched to Boves, and marched to Ferrières the next day for rest and training.

[58] Stanley Jones wrote on this date that many thought "we are bound for Servia but a regiment is always full of rumours and it really makes no difference where we fight. Servia would mean open fighting and less trenches, which would suit us better."

[59] Alwyn owned the Werner Edition of the works of L. Muhlbach, published by the New Werner Company of Akron, Ohio. These "historical romances" were written during the 19th century, and translated for this edition by Adelaide de V. Chandron.

with the ideas you got from the book. I liked the one about Eugene; I think you read it.[60] It is a splendid thing knowing that other countries have histories as well as our own. Don't forget to read up Roman or Grecian history; especially Roman as it is the start of the European history. They say the Germans are all well up in history, while our people as a whole are lamentably ignorant of all history except a smattering of their own.

We have about eight candles alight in the barn; I am in a hay mow and have been here almost a week; it might be our barn in Sombra [Ontario] only smaller; two mows and a barn floor, half of the platoon in one mow, half in the other. The farmer is away fighting in Belgium and his wife looks after things, and she is quite able to, but she doesn't much like the candles in the barn!! But it's wonderful how safe they are.

You don't see many young men round this country; it is always old men doing the farm work. I was at a restaurant the other day, and before we ate my companion asked for water to drink; how horrified the proprietor looked, and then laughed. "Water," he said. "Why, that's for fish; do you want fish to swim round in your stomach?" They drink wine here but they don't get drunk, or anyway, not as much as our people do on spirits.

I have a special kit which makes a sleeping bag, a rain coat, a blanket, and an overcoat. It would be fine up north, but I shall be lucky if I can bring it back, as everything gets lost in time. All letters are welcome. I don't suppose Danaker is round Edmonton these days.

With love to all
   from your affectionate Father
      A B-M

---

[60] L. Muhlbach, *Prince Eugene and His Times An Historical Romance* (Akron, Ohio: The New Werner Company, 1868).

LETTER 55

L/C Bramley-Moore
P.P.C.L.I.
Nov. 3rd/ 15

My dear Laura:

Many thanks for the long letter you sent me. You are all greatly improving in your writing in every respect. You see it is a good thing you have somebody to write to for practice, as it is so stupid to be able to say nothing and write nothing, and we must all practice. We don't want to say too much, and as I have found out here, we don't want to write too much!! As my letters are criticized before they reach you, and I am told they show a deplorable lack of historical knowledge! So you see how necessary all those books are, and how much more reading I must do when I get back, but alas I am afraid I may have to work! Not that we should mind work, but your father is getting old and he has got out of the way of work, and I am quite sure they won't keep me for a soldier after the war as I smile too much.

What are you going to grow up to be; very solemn or a little mischievous? As long as your mischief is good natured, I would sooner see some mischief than all solemnity, and the solemn people can be so funny without knowing it. There is a piece of poetry on a page of paper in my book of quotations about "Said I to the world," and "said the world to me." Four verses (long ones) two on each side; if you can find it I wish you would copy it and send it [to] me. I want to show it [to] a man here who can appreciate clever things.

I am sorry you have missed some letters but they have been lost. This is what happened to a playwriter named Bernard Shaw. He sent over a manuscript of a play to New York and it was sunk in the *Arabic*; he then sent another copy and it went down on the *Hesperian*; he had to send a third which I presume reached its destination.[61] So some of my letters are quite liable to have gone down.

---

[61] This probably refers to the wartime American production of *Androcles and the Lion* (1912), a satire of Christianity. Shaw's *Common Sense About the War*, published in *The New Statesman* in November 1914, had made him unpopular by this time; Shaw was denounced by many public figures for his lack of patriotism.

I like being over here in France better than drilling in England, but we are not getting any fighting here at present, so you needn't worry about me. We have one or two good old scouts who have seen a lot of fighting and still like it. They get very unhappy away from the trenches, but still in the olden days there were generally long gaps between fights, so they musn't expect to be fighting all the time. No special news; I don't know what we are going to do, but we appear to be in for a long rest.

With lots of love to all
from your loving Father
A B-M

LETTER 56

L/C Bramley-Moore
P.P.C.L.I.
Nov. 3rd / 15

My dear Dorothy:
Many thanks for all your letters. You write very nicely and I am glad you have got a seat in the Honor row. I think you and Laura are both benefiting by all that dictation we used to do and I am sure William got a good start from his reading Aesop's fables etc. It's a pity you children cannot read some of Shakespeare's plays together like Alfred and I used to; you could each take your own parts; it would do you all a lot of good. I am too poor to offer prizes just now, so you must do it for the love of knowledge! I am writing with a certain pen that Eva sent me, but I have got my fingers all over ink just like, I daresay, William sometimes gets his fingers .

I think I have told you about this barn; we are still in the same one and don't know when we are going. It has been very wet and nasty, so we were lucky not to be in the trenches in the mud. I have been keeping very warm in my nest.

I am sorry to hear the McNamaras have left Edmonton; there will be a good many changes when I come back.[62]

What do you think about the war? I asked Granny to send the quilt with the map back to you; you will never have seen it before. That was made when the South African war was on so it is a good

[62] The McNamara family lived on 98th Avenue across from the Bramley-Moore house in Edmonton.

"William's Quilt."

many years old.[63]   I am always glad to get letters.

I would sooner be in the trenches than out, as it is much more interesting. I was lucky to get over in time to see the trenches before this spell of rest started, as I would have fidgeted if I hadn't seen them. Now at least I have become acquainted with the real thing and know what it's like.

What books do you read now? Do you play games at night? Do you use all the bedrooms? I suppose you use Minnie's as that would be a warm room over the kitchen.[64]   Wouldn't she be interested if

[63] The quilt was made by Nellie Bramley-Moore on the Sombra farm in Ontario at the time of the South African War. Its design was that of a world map, with countries of the British Empire represented by red patches. Alwyn cut out these shapes for his wife to sew onto the backing. His brother, Alfred, had fought in South Africa. After the war, the quilt was sent to England, but was returned to Canada for William during the Great War, and became known in the family as "William's Quilt." Mary Anne Kinloch, his daughter, inherited the quilt about 1987. As for the instructional benefits of the quilt, Gladys Bramley-Moore later concluded that "I think it worked."

[64] Minnie was the Bramley-Moore maid in Edmonton until about 1914.

she were alive? Who did you buy your potatoes from? Did the German as usual come round? If he did, I hope you had a smile for him the same as I would; brave people don't hate brave enemies, but cowards hate them; most of our national heroes are fighters, so it is absurd to call fighters wicked; when a nation sneers at fighting, it is ready to perish and to make room for a race not ashamed of fighting; the victory goes to the best fighters and prayers are stupid. Wouldn't Hindenburg smile if he only had prayers to fight? Those trench mortars that came over at us didn't resemble prayers one bit and we respected them.

Lots of love to all from your affectionate Father
ABM
L/C Bramley-Moore
P.P.C.L.I.

LETTER 57

L/C Bramley-Moore, 1834
Nov. 7th 1915
P.P.C.L.I.

Gladys Bramley-Moore.

My dear Gladys:

I am looking for a letter from you but I suppose you are kept busy getting your lessons ready for the next day. We shall hardly know one another when we meet, and I suppose you will be shaking hands at an angle of 90 degrees!!

I am writing this in a French farm house, and I am sitting next [to] the stove, but we sleep in the barn. They don't spend much time here cleaning floors; this is a brick floor and the soldiers gave it a sluicing the other day. The farmer is away fighting and his wife runs the place. She has one little girl about your age, but the soldiers don't like her much; she spits at them!! And some of them say, "Oh, if we could only get a chance to give you a hiding." They can say what they like as the mother doesn't understand them. This is what comes of being a spoilt child; one becomes a nuisance to oneself and to everybody else.

I washed my socks and towel today. My socks are a new kind Granny knits for me; they have no heels so you can turn them round each time you put them on. I like them much better than socks with heels and I am sure they last longer as there is no constant friction in the one place to make holes.

Our Company gave a concert last night. They had what they call a bum-band; they had a biscuit tin for a drum, and all their other instruments were home-made; combs and flutes made of cardboard. Then they dressed up, some as niggers, some as girls, and some as guys and girls.[65] The girls were excellent; one of the officers fell in love with one of them, and had to be told it wasn't a real one. He is still busy making excuses they say, tho' he is such a brave and handsome officer that nobody dares joke him too much!! (I put that in so that each of the officers will think he is the one meant). We had the concert in a French school-house; the walls were covered with maps and drawings. In the afternoon we had sports; our Company was very victorious and won most of the events.

We practiced throwing bombs the other day. I hear we leave here for somewhere tomorrow. We have no idea what we are going to do next, but I hear we may leave the 27th Division and be attached to a Canadian Division.[66] I think they would sooner stay with the Division they have been with so long. I should like to go to Serbia. How do you like the quilt-map?

Lots of love to all from your affectionate Father
A. B-M
L/C Bramley-Moore
1834

---

[65] Such bands were a common military tradition; "nigger" was a term thoughtlessly used in reference to the black-face minstrel or "coon" show makeup popular among entertainers of the period.
[66] The P.P.C.L.I. left the 80th Brigade, 27th Division on 8 November 1916. It then marched to Flixecourt where it acted as an Instructional Battalion for the Third Army Officers' Training School.

LETTER 58

Nov. 7th/ 15
P.P.C.L.I.
L/C Bramley-Moore, 1834

My dear William:

I got your letter yesterday, and one from your mother. Many thanks for them. I looked over your sums and could see no mistake. I will give you a hard sum, but if you think very hard you should be able to find the answer.

The Germans have 8,000,000 soldiers. Each year they lose 1,000,000 soldiers. Each year they obtain 4,000,000 fresh soldiers. After how many years will there be only 2,000,000 soldiers left?

That is one of the reasons you do arithmetic, in order that you may be able to find out such things, but of course it has many other uses. An engineer, a surveyor and an artillery officer are all dependent upon arithmetic and higher mathematics. If one of you boys are very clever at mathematics, you might consider whether it would be worthwhile to become an engineer (civil). Different qualities are wanted in different professions, and the child's ability in this or that direction should be a determining factor in the choice of his career.

If you find my letters hard in places to understand, you must get somebody to explain them to you. You see, I can't help but think that you have grown into a big man as you now write in ink.

We are doing no fighting now, and I don't know when we will do any more. If I had known we weren't going back to the trenches, I think I would have crawled out last time I was there and seen how close I could have got to the German trenches, because just where I was there was a road through our wire entanglements, and it would have been easy; as of course in most places it is just as hard for us to get through our entanglements as for them, but I thought we were just moving to other trenches where there was more going on, so settled to wait. I used to pop my head over the top sometimes and say "Hullo, old chap, take a crack," and then bob down quickly!! You see it is rather slow, never seeing anybody at all to shoot at, and if you expect them to show a head occasionally, you must show them one once in awhile. In one place the Germans had a dummy that they stuck up, and it looked exactly like a man and deceived our fellows who tried to shoot it, but directly they shot, a bullet

"Doing My Bit Four Years" (1918),
Frank Lucien Nicolet poster reproduced from Maurice F.V. Doll,
The Poster War, Allied Propaganda Art of the First World War *(1993).*

whizzed and almost hit the man, and then they found out that it was a dummy and that just below it the Germans had a peephole through which they shot as soon as a head appeared. Of course some trenches are more dangerous than others, and I daresay in some where there are a lot of snipers it wouldn't be "safe" to look over much, but where I was before the English troops came, the French and Germans were on fairly good terms and didn't shoot at one another at all!! I shall be more careful if I get into a livelier part. I wish we hadn't left those trenches.

I do think it stupid hearing people talking about "doing their bit"; just imagine "brave Horatius" talking about doing his bit, and when he asked for volunteers to keep the bridge with him, one man saying he had done his bit and didn't see why they should expect him to do more!![67] If we ever justified the acusation that we were a nation of shopkeepers, the sneaking pitiable whine of "doing one's bit" would justify it. Why you couldn't hold back real men from fighting, for that's their business and they wouldn't think themselves very wonderful for doing what they should glory in doing. And each man should be striving to see how much he can do, not wondering whether he was doing his bit!! Tut, tut. We must get a better motto than that. You must grow up into a big brave Albertan willing to give Alberta your all, not your bit.

Lots of love, my dear boy, and trusting that you are growing wiser every day,
    from your affectionate Father
        A B-M
        L/C Bramley-Moore
        P.P.C.L.I. 1834

---

[67] Horatius Cocles, the hero of a famous poem in Thomas Babington Macauley's *Lays of Ancient Rome* (1842).

LETTER 59

Nov. 15th/ 15
Princess Patricia's C. L. I.
L/C Bramley-Moore, 1834

My dear Alfred:

I have no special news of interest as we have not been fighting lately. We have left our old Division and are still ignorant of what is going to be done with us. I had thought we were going to Servia, and there were several bets taken on the question, but it seems to be all off now, and it looks as tho' we will go back to trenches somewhere in France.

Major Gault, who was, I believe, one of the founders of the regiment, told us that although the regiment had done well in the past, it must not live on its past achievements; and that its reputation would depend on its future conduct.[68] It is no use a regiment talking of doing its bit, because it is a regiment's business to see how much more it can do than any other regiment, or how close it can get to the best regiment; of course I mean in fighting, not in drill, as if you fight well it doesn't matter how you manage to [drill]; and drill is only important in so far as it helps you to fight well. We were told of one swell regiment who had been drilled so well in peace that they thought it a disgrace to dig themselves in, and as a result they are now doing their thinking somewhere else.

Letter to Alfred, 15 November 1915.

---

[68] Alexander Hamilton Gault (1882-1958) served with the 2nd Canadian Mounted Rifles in South Africa. During the First World War, he raised and equipped, at his own expense, the P.P.C.L.I. He personally commanded his regiment, and was wounded three times in action.

I am getting a splendid book sent out to me about Napolean's Eagles, which he gave to his regiments; we have a standard with us but as a rule regiments don't carry them with them nowadays.[69] The flag in old days helped the soldier to fight well and they need something to replace it. You see, a flag is like a dog; it never scolds you so you can't get cross with it when you may be cross at people. You are always able to forget about them and imagine that it's the flag you are fighting for. The people in the old days, with their flags and eagles, weren't as stupid as some of the modern wise-ginks choose to think, and sentiment still plays a big part. I shall be sending the book of the Eagles to the Alberta Library and you can go down and read it.[70]

We are very comfortable where we are now, in a huge factory where they make carpets, oil skins and sacking. There are vats which are used for dyeing the hemp, and we have baths in them; the water is really hot and the vats are about 20 ft. long and 3 ft. wide, so we get a fine bath. We sleep and eat and live in the drying rooms; they are quite dark, and we use candles night and day. I wouldn't want them to start drying us.[71]

Lots of love to all
   from your affectionate Father
      A B-M
      L/C Bramley-Moore, 1834

---

[69] Edward Fraser, *The War Drama of the Eagles: Napoleon's Standard-Bearers on the Battlefield in Victory and Defeat from Austerlitz to Waterloo, A Record of Hard Fighting, Heroism and Adventure* (London: John Murray, Albermarle Street, W., 1912).

[70] This book was sent to the Legislature Library shortly before Bramley-Moore's death. It was accessioned by the Library as #16996 on 6 February 1922. The names and regimental numbers of his platoon mates are inscribed on the inside front cover, and his final letter is affixed inside the front cover as well. See Letters 67 and 93.

[71] The P.P.C.L.I. marched to Flixecourt, between Amiens and Abbeville, on 8 November 1915. Stanley Jones described it as "a prosperous little factory town and we have the best billets yet."

LETTER 60

Nov. 18th / 15
P.P.C.L.I.
L/C Bramley-Moore, 1834

My dear Alfred:

In your last letter you asked me for a souvenir and said that any old thing at all from the front would please you. Well, I am sending you a cap with a history. The cap belonged to Private McIsaac and a bullet went through it without hurting him at all.[72] I will get a statement from McIsaac and one from Dalby who was with him at the time.[73] They were digging themselves in when McIsaac thought he was hit, but found out the bullet had only passed through the cap. They imagine from the way it hit him that it must have been a ricochet. It happened on the day of Neuve Chapelle but in another part of the line.[74] The Germans were attacking in the endeavour to reduce the pressure at Neuve Chapelle. St. Eloi was the name of the fight and the Princess Pats gained a great reputation from the way in which they handled themselves in this engagement, but that is all ancient history.[75] Dalby and McIsaac are both in my section.

There was another man close to McIsaac when this happened but he has been killed. I have heard, though, so many interesting things about him that I will tell you what I can as you are anxious for stories of the front. His number was 1804 and we will call him by his number.[76] He used to keep to himself a lot and his comrades

---

[72] Private F. McIsaac, Reg. no. 1803, joined P.P.C.L.I. from 17th Battalion C.E.F. in December 1914. He was wounded 2 June 1916 and was struck off strength, or discharged, on 1 July 1916.

[73] Private William Dalby, Reg. no. 1724, joined P.P.C.L.I. in August 1914 and was struck off strength to Canadian Corps Infantry School on 14 August 1917. He was mentioned in dispatches. Dalby was a close friend of Alwyn's, and wrote an account of his death to Alfred on 9 May 1916. See Letter 96.

[74] The Battle of Neuve Chapelle was fought on 10-12 March 1915.

[75] The P.P.C.L.I. defended "The Mound" near St. Eloi, when it was still held by the British army during January 1915. In 1915 miners waged a vicious battle along this front, with 33 powerful mines exploded in sheeted galleries beneath a ten-acre area. On 4 April 1916, the more famous Battle of the St. Eloi Craters took place.

[76] Private B. Patterson, Reg. no. 1804; joined the P.P.C.L.I. from the 17th Provisional Battalion in December 1914; was wounded at Frezenberg, 8 May 1915, when the Regiment was decimated; was struck off service on 23 May 1915. Alwyn thought that Patterson was killed on 8 May, 1915.

didn't regard him as very sociable; though I think myself that it must have been because he was in the habit of building castles in the air and becoming oblivious to his surroundings. On one occasion he lost his rifle in the straw at his billet and his Commander, who was very angry, said he had a good mind to send him to the trenches with a button hook - and no wonder, as losing one's rifle is a crime past foregiveness; do you remember how I scolded you for dropping the axe when the wasps got after you at Trout Lake? That was because it might have been a rifle instead of an axe, and a soldier or a hunter must hang on to their rifle whatever happens. However, his rifle was found and I daresay he soon forgot the disgrace as he started dreaming of things he was going to do.

Everybody here is interested in souvenirs but it is difficult to send them away, and you cannot carry on your back a load of souvenirs. But 1804 was souvenir-mad; his pack was full of all kinds of things. Whenever he got into an empty house he rummaged every corner and added to his collection postcards, pictures and anything unusual.

As a result of his continuous collections he made the most absurd figure when he was marching. He was short and stocky, and all his pockets were crammed full of various objects. This made him look as broad as he was tall; his pockets were bulging out, and made his haversack on the one side and water bottle on the other side stick out like a load on a pack mule.

The other men were always pulling his leg and calling for 1804, saying they had found a souvenir. They tell me, but I can hardly believe it, that they would hand him empty bully beef tins and that he would pack them away. Then in the trenches he would spend hours looking over his collection and discarding the least precious, as even 1804 couldn't carry everything which took his fancy. Evidently he had a mania for acquisition and he would never refuse any necessaries (that is the term for all things served out to the soldier) whether he wanted them or not, and one man still relates with fervour how he insisted on keeping a hat far too big for him and just the right size for the other man.

And on another occasion a sergeant, who was "mucking in" with 1804 at the time, had carefully put aside a tin of strawberry jam for the trenches as another was open; he comes in to find 1804 had opened the first tin!! That Jackdaw of Rheims would have given one of his loud "caws" if he had heard the sergeant's language, and failing to find sufficient relief for his feelings in language, he took up the tin and hurled it at 1804, just missing him and splattering its contents on the wall of the billet.⁷⁷ So you see soldiers are much like children; they lose their tempers, they do careless things without thinking and throw things about and break them, but perhaps it is better to have soldiers who can get angry than alabaster saints, because I don't believe an alabaster saint would be a match for a German, and I wouldn't like a little boy to be too good, it would be uncanny. Boys and soldiers can do silly things, without being any the worse for it as long as they are brave and don't want others to fight for them.

There was another time when there was a very bad snow storm and very little shelter. 1804 was in the dugout and there wasn't room for everybody. I suppose he thought every man was looking after himself as he would have done, and he made himself as snug as he could. At last some soldier bawled him out for taking more than his share of the shelter. Out came 1804, and he wouldn't go back again. He went behind the trenches and, to quote the soldier's words, he dug himself a grave, put his oil sheet on the top, and camped in the hole. So he showed that he could have looked after himself if he had been out in the cold, and the other soldiers might have done the same instead of looking with envious eye at the inadequate shelter that existed.

On another occasion he went up to the corporal of his section (who is at my side at this moment) and said he wanted to see the officer to ask him if he could give him an opportunity to win a Victoria Cross. The corporal said, "I will attend to that." So later on the corporal told him a big lie and said that he had seen the officer and that it was all right, that there was a machine gun in the German trench opposite and that he was to "go and get it." 1804 was very pleased, but the corporal, who was afraid 1804 would be dashing right over, had to impress upon him that he must wait till the word was given, and on no account to go until all arrangements had been made. The arrangements never were made, but 1804 was ready, and even though he lost his rifle once, wore too big a hat and ate the wrong jam, who shall dare to say that the soul which dreamed of

⁷⁷ "The Jackdaw of Rheims" is the title of a poem in *The Ingoldsby Legends*, which tells how a jackdaw stole a ring from the Cardinal of Rheims, and was cursed for its act. The book was written by Thomas Ingoldsby, the pseudonym of Rev. Richard Harris Barham (1788-1845).

Victoria Crosses wasn't a credit to the British Army. And I think his story teaches the spirit, the will that is the essential to the soldier; he needs the love of glory, the desire for it. In piping times of peace one would hear references to Napoleon as the "great murderer"...; those same people are glad to have men fight for them now, and the men who fight for glory and for medals and all those trumpery vanities according to the peacelover - those are the men you want if you are going to win, and you had better learn to bear with their eccentricities than trust altogether to the prim and proper.

Poor 1804 had his head blown off on the May 8th which was the date [censored] which left the Pats with [censored] to answer one more call in place of the [censored] who answered it in the morning.[78]

Now what I have told you is all true, but as it is so close to Xmas I will just indulge in one dream like 1804 used to. I rather think that 1804 is spending his time now going from one star to another looking for souvenirs. So be very careful when you go out, and keep your eyes open for anything that may tumble down from the skies, for I know that he will fill his pack too full and some souvenirs will be dropping down. And there, away far, if you take the north star as your front, to the left nine o'clock three fingers, if you look very close, you may see him on clear nights, squatting over his pack and gloating over his souvenirs, and I daresay he keeps looking out for chances to win or find Victoria Crosses.

But of one thing I am quite sure; that 1804 isn't singing psalms and spiritual songs and that if uniformity existed in the skies before his arrival, it has been upset by the arrival of 1804, but he won't mind, as he was a companion to himself and I daresay he is just as happy by himself upstairs there, hunting for souvenirs, as the stiff old prigs are who keep themselves warm by looking at their wings.

With love to all
from your affectionate Father
ABM
L/C Bramley-Moore
1834

---

[78] These censored references probably concern the terrible toll taken on the Patricias at Frezenberg. G.W.L. Nicholson recorded that when the Patricias were relieved following this battle, their total trench strength consisted of four officers and 150 men; the day's casualties totaled 392.

You must consider this as a public letter sent to all of you children, as I want you all to keep your eyes open for 1804's souvenirs. Show this letter to Adair and Frank Walker and wish them both a Happy New Year - from me. Tell Adair he must write me a line, and that I look forward to a [*merry*] dinner on my return.

LETTER 61

Nov. 20th/ 15
P.P.C.L.I.
L/C Bramley-Moore
    1834

My dear William:

Thanks for your letters. I am glad you are keeping well and getting strong. How did you like the quilt, and do you know the names of all the countries yet, and seas. You should learn from it early, so you can show one another the different countries before you go to sleep, and before you get up in the morning. I thought it looked very grand when I looked at it in England, and I hadn't seen it for 10 or more years.

We suddenly got orders to leave the quiet place we were at, and now we are back at the front with the Canadians, and will be having our whack of the trenches again. I am glad, as I didn't want to hang around all winter doing nothing; after a good spell of trenches, then I might enjoy a rest, but I don't want a rest before we have done anything, and by far the bigger portion of our regiment are more or less recent arrivals.[79]

I shall be very glad to get your parcel when I am in the trenches, and they will be wet and cold. I haven't sent that cap off yet, as we left so suddenly, and I meant to send it from there, and now I must wait for another chance.

We had a long ride in a train; forty of us in a boxcar, but not as big as they are in America, but we all squatted down somehow or other

---

[79] Captain Jones observed that the "people of Flixecourt seemed very sorry to see us go and tears were plentiful. I shouldn't wonder if many 'happy homes' were broken up." Jones also reported that the men were transported in boxcars, "pretty crowded, forty in each, five officers to a compartment. We passed through Boulogne, Calais, Hazebrouck and detrained at Caistre where, as we pulled in a Canadian band played 'O Canada'.... The band played us three miles out here to Flêtre...."

and made ourselves comfortable. We had quite a long march to the station and a short march at the other end. I am getting my first experience of "cobbled" roads; these are roads which are paved with stones, but the surface is not smooth, and it is awfully tiring walking or driving on it. But it would be better than Edmonton mud, and the roads would be impossible if it wasn't for the stones.

The weather is getting colder and wetter. I expect to find very dirty trenches, and I daresay I won't like them as much as I did the first I went into, but the more one sees the better. I don't sleep well doing nothing, and it is a nuisance being awake at nights, but I think I will sleep good enough when we are in the trenches, tho' of course we sleep when we are relieved and have to stay awake in the trenches.

It was snowing today and the little children looked out of the window and said, "Bad for the soldiers in the trenches, but good for the 'allemands' (Germans)." I am in a little cottage writing at a table, but we sleep in a barn, but [have] lots of straw and [are] very comfortable.

Lots of love to all
from your affectionate Father
A. B-M
L/C Bramley-Moore
1834

LETTER 62

Nov. 22nd/15
P.P.C.L.I.
L/C Bramley-Moore, 1834

My dear Laura:

Thanks for your long letter which I got about two days ago. I am glad you had such a merry Hallowe'en and enjoyed yourselves. We had no fun here and I doubt if anybody knew it was Hallowe'en. We haven't been near the trenches so we had no chance to play the German tricks, but I don't think we would be allowed to play anybody tricks nowadays; we are getting so delightfully proper. There is an old lady whom I daresay you know or have met lately as you are growing big; her name is Mrs. Grundy and people say you cannot amount to much unless you conform to her liking in deportment, manner and carriage; well, the same dear old lady has a relation who is a General whom all soldiers know; his name is General Uniformity, and before we can be classed as good soldiers we have to please his taste in deportment and manners. I don't think he would like to see soldiers playing Hallowe'en tricks. We are commencing to please him immensely, I am glad to say, though you musn't believe all I say.

There is no need for you to worry about my safety, as the Germans can't get at us, and it looks as though we intended to stay here for some time. I don't know what the Sportsmen are doing, and I have written to ask. I think I have already told you all about this place, so we are only doing what we used to do in England, so it is hard to find interesting news.

I would sooner be in the trenches as time passes quicker there. Here the nights are so long and I start to sleep poorly again. How we used to sleep when we came out of the trenches; and then we would be back in again and time would fly, but now it drags.

They all tell me you have grown into a young lady; you are in a great hurry as you are not 14 yet. I am writing this in a Frenchman's house where there are two little boys. They like showing me their school books, and I was asking them questions in geography and making them show me places on the map; they would be just as noisy shouting answers as all you used to be, and each one trying to shove the others back, as a third boy was in that night. I believe I must have lost your puzzle but I thought I sent one answer.

With lots of love to all
   from your affectionate Father
      A. B-M.
      L/C Bramley-Moore, 1834

LETTER 63

Nov. 22nd/ 15
P.P.C.L.I.
L/C Bramley-Moore, 1834

My dear Dorothy:
   Thanks for your letter, which I have just received, and thank your Mother for hers. Alex McQueen happens to be in the room here as I write, and I showed him what you said about his wound etc. He wouldn't let me read it to the others, because it is all a yarn, as he has never been wounded, and good soldiers don't like a lot of silly

stories getting told when they are not true. He is in Platoon 15 so I always see him on parade, as his platoon marches next to mine.[80]

Thanks for the cuttings. Please thank everybody for the parcel; it was very nice and got here quite safe. The cake was very good, and each man in my section had a slice. I enjoyed the chocolates. Didn't your mouths water when you packed it? It is a pity postage is so heavy; I think they should give a cheap rate for parcels to soldiers, as although we are well fed and well paid people, [we] like sending things, and we like getting them.

You said that you had got the quilt, but you didn't say if you liked and admired it, and on whose bed is it put. I want it used and not put away. As by seeing it every day Gladys and William and you too will soon know all your geography without any hard work at learning. I hope you make another on the same plan. I forget if Laura was born or not when it was made. It belongs to me, I think, and I shall want it on my bed when I come back.

I get quite a lot of letters from you all, and I am pleased to get them. Do you get my letters regularly? I suppose you know they come in turns, so if one misses, it has been lost somewhere.

It is getting a long time since I came away; you will be too big to be climbing round me as you used to.

It has been cold here and we have had some snow but it has gone again. Where I live is very warm though.

If I keep telling you how I drill, you will start to think that I came over to drill and not to fight - drilling is much safer, but I would like a little fighting once in a while. My gracious, what wonderful processions they will be able to have when we all get back!! I have no more news so must close with lots of love to all.

from your affectionate Father
A. B-M.
L/C Bramley-Moore
1834

Can you read my writing?

[80] Lance Corporal Alex R. McQueen, McG 62, originally joined the 2nd University Battalion, and joined the P.P.C.L.I. as a reinforcement on 1 September 1915. He died of wounds received at Sanctuary Wood on 2 June 1916. McQueen was the son of Rev. D.G. McQueen, minister of First Presbyterian Church in Edmonton. Laura and Dorothy Bramley-Moore were close friends of his sisters. Dorothy remained close to Helen McQueen (Mrs. Charles Learmonth) all their lives.

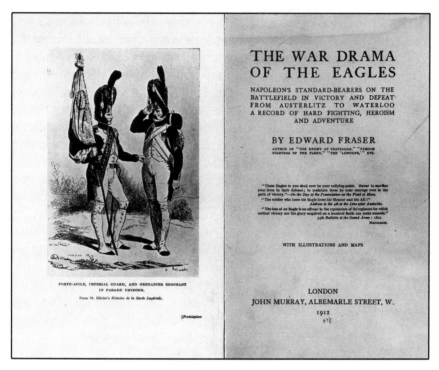

Title page of The War Drama of the Eagles *(1912)*

LETTER 64

[*The following is a handwritten note inside the front cover of book carried by Bramley-Moore and his fellow platoon members*].
Nov. 27th 1915
[*Flêtre*]
France

This book, which at present follows the fortunes of Platoon 16 P.P.C.L.I. is destined to be presented to the Alberta Provincial Library.

If found astray from its Regiment, the finder will please hand it to his Officer who is requested to forward it to the above Library.[81]

[81] This note was written by Alwyn inside Edward Fraser's *The War Drama of the Eagles* (1912). See Letter 59.

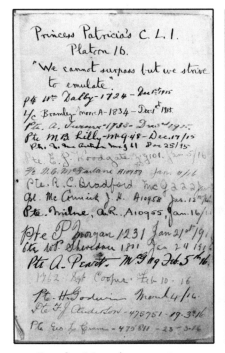 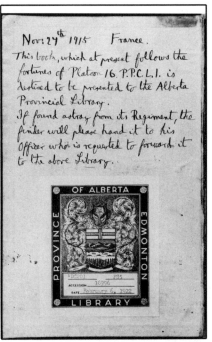

Bramley-Moore's note written inside the cover of The War Drama of the Eagles, *27 November 1915.*

The names of all the men of Platoon 16 who read the book were inscribed inside the front cover.

LETTER 65

Dec. 4th/ 15
P.P.C.L.I.
L/C Bramley-Moore, 1834

My dear Alfred:
　Your letter has just arrived; many thanks, and also thank Dorothy and Gladys for their letters. I certainly think that Gladys will soon be able to write in small letters.
　I sent your cap over, and tied a string in the holes in which the bullet went. The bullet went in at the top and came out through the flap, then striking the ground. Dalby is writing an account of it now; he was next to him (i.e. Private McIsaac). Dalby has seen a lot, and been with the regiment ever since it was made; he is very brave but modest. Dalby can't be sure which way the bullet went, but thinks

it must have hit him; probably in the cap-badge as he gave a yell, not of fear but of fury!! And dashing out of the trench, with his bayonet in his mouth, he dashed at the Huns!! This is the way these things are reported by heroes who haven't stayed long in the trenches, but you will see that Dalby, who was there, doesn't make it nearly as exciting.

We had quite a lot of fun last night over the spelling of a word. The corporal of my section insisted that the word "equanimity" was spelt "equanamity" and he dared bets, so after cautioning him, I bet with him once and then again. I did all I could to persuade him from betting wildly with other people, as we didn't want the money to go out of the section, but he couldn't be stopped and he made a lot of bets. Of course a dictionary proved him wrong and he is content to pay, though asserting that the word ought to be spelt "equanamity," and he still expects to find that select circles spell it so. This shows that there is some use in being a good speller, and still more in having a knowledge of Latin and Greek. Knowing Latin, it would be impossible to imagine, after writing it down and examining it, that it was "am," so it is a good example to you of how words are made....

Don't learn like a parrot; try to understand the reasons and you will grow up a big man, as the world is full of parrots. I do beg of you to read on your own account Greek and Roman history, as all later history is based on theirs, so you can never be in a position to understand later times without this knowledge. From the Greeks we inherit "art," using it in a broad sense, and from the Romans we inherit "laws" (jurisprudence). Other countries had arts and laws, but the one was specialized in by the Greeks and the other by the Romans. Both have helped to build up our civilization and to make man different from other animals. From the Jews [*the Judeo-Christian tradition expressed in the Bible*] we inherit superstition, and that has tended to impair the advantages we would have otherwise reaped from the Greeks and Romans. It is a good thing to bear in mind that christians themselves have labelled that age in which the church was at the height of its power as "The Dark Ages" (!!) while they talk of the "Golden Age of Augustus" before christianity arose. But you judge for yourself on these matters, only use your reason and don't repeat like a parrot either my talk or parson's talk.

The corporal on reading Dalby's account was very amused at the words - "borrowing my entrenching tool" - because McIsaac is always borrowing; he never has a mess tin, fork or spoon, and is always surprised that he hasn't. He often borrows mine, and I think he must imagine that I am an old fogey, as I don't let him forget it till I have it back. You see, up north we couldn't afford to lose things as we couldn't borrow or replace [*them*], and that habit of wanting to know I have all my belongings clings to me. I will write to Christie a little later from the trenches.[82] I got one parcel but none with cigars so far.

    Lots of love to all
        from your affectionate Father
            A B-M
            L/C Bramley-Moore, 1834

LETTER 66

France
Dec. 5th 1915

[*My Dear Alfred*]

We had been in the town of W— — — just a couple of days for the purpose of having a rest after a trip in the trenches, which at that time were very wet and muddy, when all at once we had orders to Stand-to, and were not allowed to go far from our billets, as we were liable to leave at any minute. The order stood good for two days, and on the evening of the second at 6 p.m. we were rushed off, and after a march of a few miles we halted just outside the village of V— — —. We were halted on the road for about ten minutes or so, when we got news that the Germans were advancing, and were supposed to be only a few hundred yards away. [*By this time*] the rifle fire [*began*] to increase, and the bullets were falling too close to be pleasant. Presently an order came for us to get off the road into a field and dig ourselves a protection from the enemy's fire. I had nearly finished a place for myself when a fellow in the same Section as myself by the name of MacIsaac came and dropped himself beside me, and borrowing my entrenching tool, started digging himself in. All at once he gave a bit of a cry, as he thought he

---

[82] Doug Christie was a friend of Alfred's who lived near 109th Street and 98th Avenue.

was hit; a bullet had struck his cap badge and passed through the front of his hat, and went out again without doing him any further injury. It was quite a close shave, but a miss was as good as a mile they say.

Love to all.

LETTER 67

Dec. 7th/ 15
P.P.C.L.I.
L/C Bramley-Moore, 1834
No military news except that we have issue of rum.

My dear William:

A very merry Xmas to you and a Happy New Year. This is the paper and envelope I got in the parcel; I am very glad it came as I am just out of writing paper, and they don't seem to sell this kind over here.

I used to be very fond of New Year's night when I was a boy. I can remember just a year or so before I left England how I used to put on my dress suit, and have a bowl of punch made, and very carefully welcome in the New Year. Punch is the proper drink, and if it is made right it is very good. Here we shall probably get rum for New Year's night, and the rum is excellent too. We don't get it often now as we are not suffering from the wet or cold, but I am told we will get it pretty regularly when we get into the trenches in winter.

I hear you are not going to be allowed any drink in Alberta: I am sorry, as although I hate a drunkard bothering round one, I hate still worse a lot of prigs who can only keep themselves clean because there is no mud round.[83] I don't want to live in a glass-case; you will all be so nice soon with your grandmotherly laws that you boys and girls will just sit and simper at one another saying "oh la." You won't conquer the world, my boy, if you have to run away from danger. Drink may hurt a man but so do bullets, but we musn't run away.

[83] A plebiscite on prohibition was held in Alberta in 1915, in response to the growing power of women's groups and religious organizations. When this plebiscite favoured prohibition, Premier A.L. Sifton's government enacted legislation in 1916 which restricted the sale, distribution and consumption of alcoholic beverages.

We find that a tot of rum at night is a boon and a blessing. A large number of us here, if we had to choose between a ration of rum at night or a prayer from a parson, would choose the rum, but the people at home seem to choose the prayer!! You needn't pray for your Father, my boy; I want your good wishes, not your prayers. You are starting a New Year and I hope that it will be a very happy one for you; you must learn all you can and work hard. You will have a fair start with others in the new country you are in, and if you feed your brain with knowledge, and digest it, you will be able to get to the top, but you must depend on yourself and try. I am always so pleased to hear that you are doing well, and I was proud to know that your class had voted you to be the best reader. Can you remember reading Aesop's with me? You must help Gladys when you can.

Lots of love, my dear boy, and ever so many wishes for a Happy New Year from your affectionate Father.

A. B-M.
L/C Bramley-Moore, 1834

LETTER 68

Dec. 7th/ 15
P.P.C.L.I.
L/C Bramley-Moore, 1834

My dear Dorothy:

A very merry Xmas and a Happy New Year. I should think that by the time this letter reaches you Xmas will have gone, but I hope this will reach you for the New Year. I got the parcel all right and many thanks. I saw what you had written on it. I sent you all over some trinkets some time ago; I hope you get them safe.

We are not having a very hard time of it at present; the weather has been very wet but not cold, as our billets are very cosy. Our barn is well-built and has a good roof and walls and is full of straw. I sleep very comfortably; I think it must be good sleeping in these more or less open places as I certainly keep very well.

This last week I have been orderly corporal. I have to go round and parade the sick in the morning, and be at the cook wagon at meal times to see that each platoon gets its share. Then at night I go round to the different platoons and read out the orders for the next day. Our

Company is billeted in four barns a good distance apart, one platoon in each barn, so I have a good deal of running round, and it takes me some time going round. I wrote to Jordan and told him that soldiers were so reluctant to go sick that I had to call out three times, "Anyone going sick?" and that I had heard that in other regiments they could get the soldiers to admit that they were sick by only calling out once or twice! What do you think? Perhaps I was pulling his leg. One morning I had none at all, and another morning I had ten, which was the most I had. The Doctor looks at them and if they are very ill he excuses them duty; if they are not seriously ill, he gives them medicine and light duty, which lets them off parade but leaves them liable to be called on for some fatigue work; and if he thinks there is nothing much the matter with them, he gives them medicine and duty and they then go on all parades. Naturally, the men are glad to know that they are well and strong and fit for duty. That last sentence may be a lie; you must think whether little boys and girls always like to go to school, or whether they don't at times tell their Mother that they are too ill to go and she doesn't believe them; are they glad then or not? Soldiers are just like children, so you can figure out for yourself the truth.

Lots of love, dear Dorothy, and my best wishes for a very happy and prosperous New Year

>from your affectionate Father
>A. B-M.
>L/C Bramley-Moore, 1834

LETTER 69

Dec. 7th/ 15
P.P.C.L.I.
L/C Bramley-Moore

My dear Laura:

A very merry Xmas to you and a Happy New Year. I got the parcels that you have all sent to me and they were very welcome. I am now hard at work writing a New Year's letter to each of you, and then this afternoon I shall enjoy the two cigars I have left; they are very good indeed.

One man in my section was wounded last March and was sent to England. He was on a train, and met a lady from Canada who started chatting with him. She asked if he got news from Canada, and he casually answered that he didn't get much, and that he would like to see a Canadian newspaper. Later he had to go back to the hospital, and one day, to his surprise, the orderly brought him in 67 letters! The lady had written to the Montreal Star and mentioned his name. His name was Robinson, and I think all the Robinsons in the world thought they ought to write, and ever so many others. When he left the hospital and went back to Shorncliffe Camp, the man at the pool office said "Oh, you're the wretch we are looking for with a club, eh? Look at this," and he showed him three huge mail sacks all filled with newspapers addressed to him!!! He could only answer some of the letters, and had to write to the newspaper and ask it to thank them for him, and mention that he was quite well now, and hint that he had sufficient correspondence; but he still keeps up correspondence with quite a number.

A great fuss is made about the soldiers, eh! I don't see that it is anything so very wonderful to be willing to fight for one's country; a lot of men usually want to fight if somebody else tells them the truth, by saying what stupid fools they are, so surely they ought to be willing to fight if their country is at war. We are very well fed and extremely well paid for soldiers. I doubt if in the whole history of the world there were ever such well-paid soldiers as the various Colonial soldiers.

Please wish Mr. and Mrs. Hopkins, and Mrs. Johnson, and Gladys, a Happy New Year from me; tell them that I can't promise to write as I have too many people to write to, so it is hard work when there is no special news, as I like a letter to be reasonably interesting. Did you get a long letter I wrote about a soldier number 1804? I hope you did and that you like it. This is the fourth letter I have just written and I must still write to Alfred and your Mother. I need a brain like Munchausen or DeRougemont....[84] Do you read at all those history books we used to do dictation from? I bet you don't, but you must.

    Lots of love, my dear Laura
       from your affectionate Father
         A. B-M.
         L/C Bramley-Moore, 1834

---

[84] Baron Munchausen was a famous character created by Rudolf Erich Raspe in *Baron Munchausen's Narrative of his Marvelous Travels and Campaigns in Russia* (1785). His name is synonymous with exaggerated personal memoirs of derring-do. Michel Nicolas Balisson de Rougemont (1781-1840), was a prolific French dramatist, novelist and journalist.

LETTER 70

Dec. 7th 1915
P.P.C.L.I.
L/C Bramley-Moore, 1834

My dear Alfred:
A very merry Xmas to you and a Happy New Year. I got the parcel and have enjoyed the cigars. I wrote to you the other day, so this need only be a short letter carrying my New Year's greeting. If William hasn't had any souvenir yet, I will send him one; I thought perhaps he would have one of those trinkets I sent some time ago. There must be no quarrelling about things sent over, and if one gets more than their share they must be willing to divide with the others. Some may get lost on the road, so the lucky ones must divide with the unlucky. They tell me that I am quite likely to get my periscope smashed by a German bullet in the trenches. When I do, I will send it over as a souvenir. You can bet your boots that I won't try to let them hit it, as it is far too useful and it will be difficult to replace. It would be a nuisance, eh, if it was necessary to go and capture a German trench in order to get a new periscope!! I saw a long time ago in the papers about a man who had to kill eight Germans before he could get a pair of boots to fit him! I have been looking for him, but haven't met him yet; I naturally expected to find him in the Pats, as they are such great fighters, but perhaps he is modest, and perhaps he has forgotten the incident and won't remember it till he has to think about getting a new pair of boots.

Quite a large draft has just joined us.[85] A big ceremonial parade was held and they were introduced to the colors. The colors were marched along in front of the draft at a very slow pace while the draft presented arms to them. Then the Colonel addressed them, and told them that they had to stick to the colors at all costs.[86] We are, I think, the only regiment here which carries colors. You see we were given our colors by the Princess Patricia, and we must give them a baptism of war. There is a hole or two in them now from

---

[85] The first draft from the 3rd University Company arrived in camp on 5 December 1916.

[86] Lt. Col. H.C. Buller, DSO, resumed command of the Regiment on 7 December 1916; on 16 December, the colors were paraded to say farewell to Lt. Col. R.T. Pelly, who had been appointed to command the 8th Royal Irish Regiment.

The Path of Duty 97

Richard George Matthews' sketch of Major Arthur Hamilton Gault, DSO, P.P.C.L.I. Original in Canadian War Museum. (PA-7218, National Archives of Canada.)

shells. I like colors, and think they are a fine thing to have. You can take a dislike to a man or a commander, but you can't take a dislike to your standard, and you can buck up when you think of it even if you don't worship your leader. But we have a fine fellow in the organizer of this regiment, Major Gault; I have never heard one word against him, and I think he's a real man and would sooner be fighting than commanding all the time. He was wounded but is back and he won't [be] looking for safe jobs at home.[87]

Very best wishes, for a Happy and Prosperous New Year from your affectionate Father
ABM
L/C Bramley-Moore
1834

LETTER 71

Dec. 10/ 15
P.P.C.L.I.
L/C Bramley-Moore, 1834

My dear Laura:
I wrote to all of you about 10 days ago, at a guess, and I sent a picture post card to all later. Did you get them? And did you get the trinkets I sent? I have just sent to William a Canadian cap badge which I traded for; he [*the owner*] wanted to trade so I did, and I

[87] Captain Jones writes that the regiment "had a parade in 'Hollow Square' with our colours, to receive the draft and to impress upon them their responsibilities. Just as we were all ready standing at attention, who should walk on the field but Colonel (H.C.) Buller come to take over command! In spite of having lost an eye in the last heavy battle, he has the wonderful loyalty and courage to return and carry on with the old regiment."

Princess Patricia's Canadian Light Infantry badge.

thought William might like it as it has been at the front, and is rather a nice one I think.

I got a plum pudding from Granny the other day, so I and Corporal Neale set out with it, bought two young roosters and went to a small cottage, invited some friends and had a feast, helped out by cigars and coffee.[88] Dalby was one of our party; I have mentioned him before, as he wrote an account of McIsaac's cap. We drink a lot of coffee here.

We have been here some time but may move any day into the trenches. I am interested to find out how muddy they are, as we have had a lot of wet weather lately.

The farm buildings here are built in a square surrounding the barn yard; the house is always built either just next or as part of the other buildings. Then the yard is paved with bricks, while in the centre is a hole about 4 or 5 ft. deep covering more than half the yard, where the manure is thrown. On dark nights strangers are liable to fall in: I did once, and I have seen other fellows do so, but you wouldn't get hurt, tho' you might get very muddy and dirty.

Today our battalion is playing a football match with some other battalion. I don't have much news when I stay so long in one place, and when I write in a green envelope I mustn't speak about military matters.

I hear you have grown taller than your Mother. Take interest in your work and make use of your time while you are young. I have

---

[88] Corporal G. Neale, Reg. no. 1784, joined the P.P.C.L.I. in September 1914. He was wounded 11 April, 1915 and 15 September 1916. He was struck off service with the rank of sergeant on 20 September 1916.

never been told if you play that "name" game in the evenings, and have you still got a set of Halma?[89]

Lots of love to all
    from your affectionate Father
        Alwyn

LETTER 72

Dec. 16th/ 15
P.P.C.L.I.
L/C Bramley-Moore, 1834

My dear Dorothy:

Many thanks for [your] letters. The Christmas parcels are arriving and we get lots of sweets, cakes and cigars. Bob Edwards of the Calgary Eye-opener, sent a box of cigars to the Alberta University boys.[90] The people at home are all very kind to us. I wrote a French letter the other day to the little boy whose address I sent over to you.

We always try to find out a secluded cottage, if we can, when we seem to be staying long in one place; and then if it is close enough we can slip over to it and shave and wash in the mornings, as there is never much convenience for washing in farm yards. It is all right when you are alongside a stream or creek, but where there is only a pump you can never find an empty dish to wash in, as dishes are so few, and men so many.

I take the sick to the doctor every morning and have to walk about a mile and a half each way; the sick don't like it very much, so it helps to keep them well.

---

[89] Halma was a popular board game of strategy, played on 256 squares with 19 little "men" similar to chess pawns for each player. These men were grouped in "yards" of 13 squares enclosed by a black line in each corner. The object was to get men out of a yard and diagonally across the board into the yard of the opponent. Halma is a Greek word which means "leap," and the moves are accomplished by "steps" and "hops." There is no "taking" of men in Halma, but the objective is to move as swiftly as possible across the board into the opponent's yard.

[90] Robert Chambers Edwards (1864-1922), or "Eye-Opener Bob," was a Scottish immigrant who arrived in western Canada in 1894. He edited newspapers there until 1909, when he moved to eastern Canada. In 1911 he returned, and edited and published papers until his death. He was elected as an Independent M.L.A. in 1921. His most famous paper was the *Calgary Eye-Opener*, which ran from 1911 until 1923.

We are having an easy time here, but it won't be so easy soon. We have been issued our fur jackets. They are all colours, and we do look like Eskimos; mine is a white one, a lambskin I would think; it is very light and has no sleeves, as that made them too clumsy. We ought to be warm enough, but it is not cold alone we fear, but cold and wet. If it kept cold and dry, it would be a cinch for us, as the cold is trifling compared to what we are accustomed to in Canada. I have an army sweater, just the same as that one of mine that your Mother sometimes wears. I keep it on at nights, unless [the] weather is very warm. My blanket, which was part of a Kitchener's Kit given to me by my Uncle Leighton, has a pocket for my feet, so they can't get uncovered at nights.[91]   I couldn't see Alfred in the picture post card William sent me.

With love to all
   from your affectionate Father
      Alwyn

LETTER 73

Dec. 26th/ 15
P.P.C.L.I.
L/C Bramley-Moore, 1834

My dear William:

I must drop you a line tho' I am very tired, but you might wonder if there was a long gap. It's not so easy writing now, as we work harder and our quarters are not so comfortable. It is mud, mud everywhere.[92]

I am so glad to hear that the things I sent came all right; I will soon try to send more souvenirs. I hear you are well up in your work; I hope you stick to it, and in a few years you will be reading all those books in the den. I shall write to Gladys tomorrow or the next day. I wrote you all a letter not so long ago.

We had lots of plum puddings on Xmas. Major Gault's mother sent every Pat here a 1 lb. plum pudding and they were very good,

[91] Leighton Jordan was a brother of Alwyn's mother.
[92] The Regiment moved to La Clytte on 19 December 1915 and garrisoned the Mt. Kemmel defences. It spent most of its time working in the trenches. It was attached to the 7th Brigade, with the Royal Canadian Regiment, the 42nd Battalion, and the 49th Battalion on 22 December 1915.

One of the souvenirs sent home by Bramley-Moore. This little German helmet charm was only about a half inch across.

and there were cigarettes and tobacco. I have acknowledged all the parcels I have had from you, so I think that your Xmas parcels haven't come yet.

What sort of a Xmas did you have? And what kind of a New Year are you going to have? I like New Year's day, and I think it is a good day for all of us to make up our minds to succeed in whatever we may be doing.

We are forming up trenches, and where we wash we see the shells fall in the firing line. I like to hear them whizz over; you seem to hear them all the way but you can't see them, tho' you can see the trench mortars which come quite slowly.

Your poor Serbians seem to have disappeared from the map.[93]
How do you like the quilt, and are you good at geography?
Good night, my little man. I am so tired.
With love to all
    from your affectionate Father
        A. B-M.

LETTER 74

Dec.27th/ 15
P.P.C.L.I.
L/C Bramley-Moore, 1834

My dear Gladys:
Many thanks for your letter and for your reports; I am glad to see you are getting on so well at school. How will you like it when I come back and you have to read to me at home like William used to.

---

[93] When the Austro-German offensive pushed the Russian army back to a line over 200 miles east of Warsaw, Bulgaria was encouraged to join the Central Powers to crush Serbia and Montenegro. The Serbian army was rolled back to the Adriatic, and when Greece repudiated its treaty with Serbia, the Allies felt powerless to intervene.

I had just finished my letter to William last night when I got the letter from you and William and your Mother. Tell William that I think he should take more pains with his letters and not have so many scratches out. [*Here Bramley-Moore jokingly wrote the word "and," and scratched it out*]. When I was a boy at school, we had to write home every week, and our letters were looked over by the school mistress, and they had to be written just so. It all helps one in one's education, writing and reading letters. I was glad to see all your reports.

I hope you all had a merry Xmas and are going to have a happy New Year. You didn't see me at all during 1915.

I am glad to get to my bed early out here; I am always in bed by 8:30 and sometimes by 7. I am writing this in bed.

I have had lots of plum pudding. Granny sent me out a small tin of turkey and a big tin of tongue which had no label on, which I kept for Xmas thinking it was turkey! I passed it round as turkey, and we all imagined it was turkey, tho' we thought it was rather carefully hidden.

Lots of love to all
from your affectionate Father
Alwyn

LETTER 75

Jan. 2nd / 16
P.P.C.L.I.
L/C Bramley-Moore, 1834

My dear Alfred:

The New Year has started and I hope it will bring luck to all of you, but as a rule luck comes to those who try to help themselves, so don't sit down and wait for luck.

I have no very grand news. We have been digging trenches not far behind the firing line and we could easily see where the shells kept falling from the gun. Lots of mud in the trenches; we expect to be in the firing trenches in a few days; I would sooner be in them than fussing round as we have been doing for so long.

On one occasion when we were returning to our quarters from the trenches shells started falling all around us, and one [*fell*] very close in front of us; it made the march interesting. You hear them whizz along over your head and you can tell if they are going to drop close. You know the "ping" of a .22 bullet; well, a shell just makes a much louder whizz, and you can almost follow the noise as it cleaves through the air.

I don't expect big fighting till nearer spring as there is too much mud. I don't think we have seen the biggest battle yet, and there ought to be some tremendous ones in 1916.

I spent a very pleasant New Year's Day; we were back in comfortable barns for New Year's Eve.[94] We are in bed by 8 or 8.30 p.m. Have you had [*the McIsaac*] cap yet? I saw Bennett the other day; the young fellow from Kitscoty who used to work for Ginn.[95]

Lots of love to all from your affectionate Father
ABM

LETTER 76

820 Dorchester Street, West
Montreal

Dear William:
Delighted to get your letter enclosing the ages of your brother and sisters. In your next give us the dates of all your birthdays.

Yes I shall certainly come and see you before you graduate as a doctor. How would you have liked it if just as you were about to start on your helping of nice fat turkey someone rushed in and said "Dr. William is wanted right away without a moment's delay." And then when you have just got tucked nicely up in a warm bed on a cold blowy night the telephone should ring and a voice should say, "Dr. William, I want you to come over right away and see my baby. He is cutting his teeth and also cutting up some awful." Then you would say, "Oh, I wish I was a preacher."

Are you getting on well at school? What are you studying now? I started learning Latin at 7 and Greek and French at 8.

---

[94] The Lord Strathcona's Horse relieved the Patricias on New Year's Eve, allowing them to return to Corps reserve in Flêtre.
[95] Probably this was C. M. Bennett, Reg. no. 411024, who joined P.P.C.L.I. from 1st University Battalion on 28 July 1915, and was struck off strength to the Royal Field Artillery with rank of lieutenant on 23 November 1915; Ginn was a neighbour at the Kitscoty homestead.

And since the boys nowadays say they are much smarter than we used to be, I expect you are learning Japanese and Russian, aren't you?

Last time we saw Uncle Mostyn he said he thought he had heard you talking Double Dutch. Is that so?

Lots of love. Write again soon.

Your affectionate Uncle Alfred.[96]

LETTER 77

Jan. 8th/ 16
P.P.C.L.I.
L/C Bramley-Moore, 1834

My dear Laura:

I got a letter from you the other day; many thanks. I think I told you that I got the parcel with Xmas cake and the soap and the cards etc. I like that kind of soap and the cards are very nice. I played bridge with them the other night, tho' I don't play cards much now myself; I find I can generally pass the time writing, reading or resting. That is one thing about this life, that one lies down and doesn't sit down much, and you know that I used to like to lie down. In a barn with lots of straw one rests very comfortably, and of late I have slept splendidly. I haven't felt a bit cold for ever so long, and I don't mind waking up several times in the night, as it doesn't seem to disturb my rest. I am glad there are no rats to bother us here. I hear that there are plenty in this district, but I haven't seen them.

I must have made a mistake if I put Dec. 20 instead of Nov. 20 on William's letter. The boys mentioned in your letter were the same as those in Gladys's. Have you written to them? You must get Mrs. Hopkins to help you write a letter. I got such a nice letter from them in French and I sent it to Granny. I will ask her to send it on. They wrote very tidily.

I like being in the trenches as that is what I came to see.

[96] Dr. Alfred A. Bramley-Moore was a younger brother of Alwyn's. Born in 1881, he immigrated to Canada after the South African War. He took a degree at McGill University, and practiced for many years at Victoria Hospital, with an office on Sherbrooke Street. He became one of Montreal's most prominent opthamologists.

Did Christie get the letter? I write two at a time and in turn, so if they don't turn up they must get lost in the mail.

Lots of love to all
> from your afectionate Father
>> A. B-M.

LETTER 78

Jan. 8th / 16
P.P.C.L.I.
L/C Bramley-Moore, 1834

My Dear Dorothy:

Thanks for your letter. You asked me a lot of questions but I can't remember them all.

I like the trenches all right, and I prefer being out here to camp in England. We march a lot and the roads are very hard on one's feet, and they may not be able to stand it for ever. It makes a big difference when the roads are nice and smooth and broad. Where they are narrow you have to squeeze to one side in the mud to let the motor lorries pass by, as they of course must keep on the hard road; and then those in front, whom the lorry has passed first, get back on the road earlier than the back platoons, and the back ones have to hurry their pace to catch up.

Marching with the heavy pack on your back is no joke; just now I am leaving everything behind, at a house, that I can possibly manage without, as I expect to return here later. If we stay long in a district, I like to find a cottage where I can slip over to and wash and shave in comparative comfort. So far I have been pretty lucky.

The days will be getting longer quickly now and winter soon will be over, tho' so far I couldn't call what we have had here winter. We had a good bit of snow before we moved up here, but I don't think they often get snow here.

You will be having so many letters from me you will be getting tired of them. I got your report. How did you get on with your acting at the Empire.[97] I am sorry to hear you are not well just now and hope this letter finds you all right again. Poor Clifford has been terribly ill

---

[97] The Empire Theatre was one of the largest vaudeville theatres in Edmonton during the First World War. It also hosted student productions during this time.

with meningitis. There may be a gap before [the] next letter comes.[98]
A. B-M.

LETTER 79

Jan. 18 / 16
P.P.C.L.I.
L/C Bramley-Moore, 1834

My Dear William:
    I am writing in a tent under great difficulties, so you must excuse [this] poor letter. I will try and send better letters when I can get back to a friendly house. We are in a camp of tents for one or two days, and then we go back to the trenches again.
    I have had a very bad heel, and it is going to take some trouble to get it well. Everybody is always so suspicious of everyone else shamming, that you have to wait until your foot gets very bad before you can rest up to cure it. Can you read my writing or do you have to have it read to you?
    I have been back to the trenches again; there was a lot of artillery fire going on, but we sent over more shells than they did.[99]
    I got a long and newsy letter from Frank Walker.
    It is raining hard now but it has been fine, and it was drying up a bit but now it will become bad again. Trenches need all the time to be rebuilt or they would be mud to your neck. They give us lots of work to do, but I like it when I am well, and I like to work where I can see the shells falling. Our last barn near the firing line was ever so cosy; we used to go from it to the firing trench each day and do some work and then return. Shells used to fall on all sides of our barn, but they were trying to locate our batteries not our barns.[100]

    [98] The Regiment left Flêtre on the morning of 9 January 1916 and marched to relieve the 4th Battalion, C.E.F., at Wood Farm, Dranoutre. Three days later, it moved into the front line on the right of Kemmel, where it undertook some sustained drainage work in the trenches. Heavy shelling occurred on 15-16 January, 1916. The regiment was relieved by the 42nd Divisional Reserve on 16 January.
    [99] The War Diary reports that the artillery exchange was particularly fierce between 14 and 16 January 1916.
    [100] In contrast, Agar Adamson described conditions in this section: "The trenches are full of mice and rats, the stench in places is awful, and even chloride of lime won't keep it down. The back of the trench is a mass of marked and unmarked graves."

I am so uncomfortable writing that I shall wait to write to Gladys. I hear Alfred got the cap; did he like it? Do you like Scott's Emulsion?[101] Thanks for letters. I have just got short ones from you Gladys, Laura and Dorothy.

Lots of love to all
    from you affectionate Father
        A. B-M.

LETTER 80

Jan. 30th / 16
P.P.C.L.I.
L/C Bramley-Moore, 1834

My Dear Alfred:

Many thanks for the letters; I think I have had one or two from you lately. It is longer than usual since I have written as we have [been] marching around different places at the trenches, and I wanted to wait till I got back to pen and ink if possible.[102] For a long time I had a sore heel but it is all right now. Once it made the whole of the calf of my leg swell and become one hard lump; I thought I must have got it poisoned somehow, but it gradually disappeared. It was terribly painful on one march, but I thought of the creed that teaches that we must be strong if we are to be reckoned to be fit to be masters of this earth; the weak are to be despised, and therefore we must hide from others when we feel weak, and appear strong even when we are ill. I think it is pleasanter for other people if we hide as much as possible

One of the souvenirs sent home by Alwyn Bramley-Moore.

---

[101] A patent medicine.
[102] The Patricias relieved the 42nd Battalion between 20 and 24 January 1916, had a "quiet" tour of duty, and returned to Brigade reserve at Wood Farm. On 29 January, 1916 it returned to Corps reserve at Flêtre.

one's own ailments. We must never ask for pity; pity is the same as an insult.

Did Christie get the letter I sent him? I am glad you got the cap and things. If I can, I will get hold of some other souvenirs.

Some shells came very close to our dugout, and it wasn't strong enough to stop them if they [had] hit it. I was just straining the water off some potatoes when one came down a few feet beyond me. It is wonderful how many shells can fall without hurting anybody; it seems like terrible waste. The trench mortars are worse than most of the shells, but if you are looking you can dodge them. Our dugouts are not strong enough to stop them.

My periscope is in fine shape, but the Germans don't show up in these trenches as they used to at the first ones I was in. We had two or three periscopes shot through. The trenches are quite close to one another. In places the Germans have their sandbags painted all the colours of the rainbow. They neglect nothing.

Lots of love to all
    from your affectionate Father
        Alwyn

LETTER 81

Feb. 5th / 16
P.P.C.L.I.
L/C Bramley-Moore, 1834

My dear Laura:

I asked them to send books over to you all from England, and I hear that you have got them. You must regard them as birthday presents; tell me exactly what they were like, the books. You have had two birthdays now in my absence; I won't be knowing [you] when I get back.

It has been cold and nasty here but today is much pleasanter. We have been this last week away from the trenches but we go back again tomorrow.

I got a long letter from Hiram Miller full of Lloydminster news.[103] A Gilchrist in the 49th said he would like to see me; I think he must be one of the Islay Gilchrists; I shall probably run across him as the

---

[103] Hiram Miller was a business associate and family friend.

49th works with our Battalion.[104] We had a Football match the other day with the R.C.R. (Royal Canadian Regiment).[105] Several of our companies were paraded and compelled to go to look on; they were very cross about it and a lot of them cheered and boosted for the RCRs! There were no R.C.R.s looking on, as I've heard that they wouldn't come. Both regiments had had a long route march in the morning. They never want to leave us alone; they don't seem to understand that rest consists in getting away from them all for awhile. I just like to wander off anywhere on my lonesome and get into a cottage and rest or write. In the summer one will be able to lie out of doors in a wood or hedge row. This country will look beautiful in the spring and summer.

Lots of love to all
from your affectionate Father
ABM

LETTER 82

Feb. 5th / 16
P.P.C.L.I.
L/C Bramley-Moore, 1834

Dear Dorothy:

I have got very little news to give. Tomorrow or the next day I will be close to the shells again as we are just finishing a week's rest.[106] They don't let one rest much tho', and in some ways it is more tiresome having to do silly old drill that you have done dozens of times than to listen to the booming of guns and whizzing of shells which anyway create excitement. I daresay we may be having more exciting times in the trenches soon, tho' they have been

---

[104] The Gilchrists were friends of the family who lived near Islay, Alberta, northwest of the Kitscoty homestead.

[105] The P.P.C.L.I. was brigaded together with the 49th Battalion, C.E.F. and the Royal Canadian Regiment in the 7th Infantry Brigade, 3rd Canadian Division. The 7th Brigade held a "sports" at Mont des Cats, in which the Patricias' transport won 2 first prizes and 3 second prizes. Two days earlier, a Battalion sports was attended by the Duke of Connaught, whom Alwyn, as a Member of the Provincial Parliament, and his wife had met at the reception in Edmonton when he visited as Governor-General in 1912.

[106] The Regiment marched to Locre on 6 February 1916; it relieved the 31st Battalion in the Kemmel trenches the next day.

exciting enough for some already.

When we are not actually fighting, only those soldiers who are very erect, or who would be excellent dancers, are in favour with the authorities, but I don't know if the dancing men will be the best at real fighting. Our Sergeant, who is not a dancing man, but who has proved his bravery again and again before the enemy under fire, very nearly lost command of his platoon when it looked as tho' we were going to spend some long time swanking far from the fighting; but when they suddenly got orders to return to the fighting area, he was left in command. They seem to prefer in the army a coward with erect shoulders to a brave man with round ones.

I like getting a meal on the outside; they then generally consist of fried eggs and chipped potatoes and coffee. Everybody drinks coffee here, so you scarcely ever see tea.

My heel has got quite well again, but I am tormented by lice. I wash hard enough against them but I think they have got into my woollen sweater, and I can't dispense with it. Your tar-soap was excellent; I still have one cake untouched. They have got to be very careful of paper in England now and not waste any.

With lots of love to all
    from your affectionate Father
        A. B-M.

LETTER 83

Feb. 9th / 16
P.P.C.L.I.
L/C Bramley-Moore, 1834

My Dear William:
    Thanks for [*your*] letters. By now I hope that weather is warmer over with you; it has never been very cold here yet this winter. Last night was about as cold as any night, but we were in a capital barn and very snug in lots of straw. I have one blanket; half goes under me and half over, and then I put my overcoat over my feet and as far up as it will reach; next to that I place my skin jacket. I take off my tunic and socks and cap, and keep everything else on. I have a woollen helmet, but I have never used it except for my head to lie on. I would be as snug as could be if animals didn't bite at night!!

My comrades tell me I am getting thin, but I am feeling much better lately. My feet are all right at present, and I think I have quite got over the slight attack of grip that I had.

At present I am away from my platoon, as I am taking a 10 day course at a defensive gas school. You would think us funny objects in our smoke helmets; I wouldn't want to have to wear one for an hour or two, tho' it is possible that one might have to. It is quite a change being amongst new faces, and tho' we work it feels like a real rest. They say that the Germans keep putting their men from one regiment to another, and I should say it was a good plan, as it seems to wake one up. That is why in holiday time people should trade visits and not just go away all together. You want new faces as well as new scenery; and then you are all cheerful when you meet again. Next holidays your Mother should pack you all off to different farms and go to one by herself, then you would be getting the full benefit of change.

Lots of love to all
    from your affectionate Father
        A. B-M.

LETTER 84

Feb. 13th / 16
P.P.C.L.I.
L/C Bramley-Moore, 1834

My Dear Alfred:

Not much news to give you in this letter. The weather has been rather unpleasant lately, but as I am at this Gas School I am sheltered from its discomforts. I shall be back with my platoon in a day or two, and shall be glad to be with them, though this has been a change of course, and without any change it tends to become monotonous.

Did you like Muhlbach's stories? I had only read a few of them. You should read some of the articles in the "Great Event" series on the bottom shelf, and be sure to read some Greek and Latin History. To start history with the discovery of Canada is fearfully stupid; history teaches us about the struggles, successes and failures of countries, and therefore you want to read the history of other countries in order to learn from their experience. It doesn't matter whether a certain event took place in 1913 or 1914 or 1757 or 1758, but it is important to know whether a country benefited by conquering other countries, or by refraining from foreign intercourse; whether it is better for a country to develop agriculture at the expense of commerce or vice versa. That is the object of history, to assist us in coming to a decision on these points with some experience as a guide to help us.

What do you think of the war? I wonder what Minnie would think?

I hope you are not going to join "Anti-German" leagues or such things; I don't think the soldiers who fight would join as much as those who stay behind. They fight hard enough to suit us and a good fighter exacts admiration.

I shall be glad to get home as I have been away now a long time, but I don't see much chance; it is lasting longer than most people expected. This should be a busy spring. Did the roses that were left out winter all right?

With lots of love to all
  from your affectionate Father
    A. B-M.

LETTER 85

Feb. 14th/ 16
P.P.C.L.I.
L/C Bramley-Moore, 1834

My Dear Children:

I have copied these sayings from the copy-book of a little French school-girl 8 years old named Judith Couchee. Each morning at school they write down a thought (pensée) for the day. You will notice that these thoughts never make any reference to any god; christians try to make out that "goodness" is dependent upon belief in and prayers to their god, or if not theirs at least to some god. No god is necessary. No race could exist for long which developed qualities hurtful to the race; good qualities are mechanically necessary to a race, and experience is the guide that teaches us to distinguish between good and bad customs.

Samedi		22 Janvier 1916
Pensée	-	Fuiyez toujours les occasions de mal faire. [*Always flee occasions to do bad.*]
Lundi	-	Celui qui passe sa vie dans l'oisiveté se prepare à une vieillesse penible. [*Those who spend their life in idleness will suffer a hard old age.*]
Mardi	-	L'amour filial est le premier des devoirs. [*Filial love is the first of obligations.*]
Mercredi	-	La politesse du riche le pare mieux que ses plus beaux habits. [*The courtesy of the rich protects them better than their most beautiful clothing.*]
Jeudi	-	La bienfaisance consiste dans le soulagement des misères humaines. [*Doing good consists of relieving human suffering.*]
Samedi	-	Ayons pour les autres l'indulgence. On devient facilement semblable à ceux que l'on approche. [*Show indulgence for others. One often becomes what one criticizes.*]
	-	L'avare perdi-tout en voulant trop gagner. [*The greedy lose everything in wishing to gain all.*]
	-	On pardonne aux enfants qui se repentent sincerement. [*One pardons in children what one sincerely repents oneself.*]
	-	L'ingratitude la plus odieuse est celle des enfants envers leurs parents. [*The most odious ingratitude is that of children towards their parents.*]
	-	Plus on aime quelqu'un moins il faut le flattre. [*The more one loves a person the less one needs to flatter them.*]

- Soyons modestes comme la violette.
  [*Be as modest as the violet.*]

- Le travailleur gagne sa vie. Le paresseux vole la sienne.
  [*The worker gains his life. The lazy lets his own slip away.*]

- Le fruit du travail est le plus douce des plaisirs.
  [*The fruit of work is the sweetest of pleasures.*]

It is not necessary to agree with all these sayings, but if we disagree, we are compelled to think about the matter and have reasons for differing. You are all liable to be caught more or less badly in the christian web, but I would like to protect you from the worst effects which ensue from an irrational acceptance of belief in gods. Knowledge is the heirloom of the elect; it separates them from the herd. Seek for knowledge and taste of its fruits. The christian view on knowledge is shown by their story about Adam bringing sorrow into the world because he ate the apple of knowledge.

Trusting these remarks may cause one at least to think.
From yours affectionately,
 Alwyn Bramley-Moore

LETTER 86
Feb. 20th / 16
P.P.C.L.I.
L/C Bramley-Moore, 1834

My Dear Laura:
 Many thanks for [*your*] letter, which I got on my return to my regiment. I was just wondering who it was had sent me this paper when your letter came and mentioned it. It is nice paper.
 I hear you are taller than Gladys Johnson.[107] I shall be surprised when I see you all. Which of the upstair rooms are used for sleeping

---

[107] The Johnson family lived in Lloydminster and later moved to Edmonton. Their eldest daughter, Gladys, was a little older than Laura Bramley-Moore.

in? When will you be ready to go to High School? I got a letter from Mrs. Johnson which I will answer shortly. Give her and Gladys my best wishes.

We have just been inoculated again; this time they put the serum in our chests. They didn't take long; a long line of men ends almost as fast as they can walk by. One man paints them with iodine, and another two men pierce them, and away they go. My chest is starting to feel sore, but by resting awhile I don't suppose it will trouble me, and we are back in reserves for a few days, so we have an opportunity for rest.

I saw in a newspaper that Frank Walker had enlisted as a private. He told me that he thought he might get the job of transport officer in some regiment; he is entitled to it, I am sure.

Have you heard any news of Major Anderson? I hear he is returning to Edmonton to raise a battalion; let me know where he is and what he is doing. He escaped from Germany, and all manner of different stories circulate as to his adventures. He was a nice man.

We lose a few men in the trenches once in a while; the Germans have some good snipers; one man got hit and killed through a sandbag.[108] They were aiming at a periscope or something they thought they saw above the parapet, and just missed, I suppose, and got this poor fellow. Of course they wouldn't know they had hit anybody, so I daresay one rarely can tell whether one has hit a man or not, and it is very difficult to be sure, especially if nobody is watching your shot through a periscope.[109]

With lots of love to all
   I remain
      Your affectionate Father
         A. B-M.

---

[108] The War Diary indicates that two men were killed by snipers the previous day. The German snipers were inaccessible in their "Fort", "which is very strong, [and] needs smashing up with big guns."

[109] The Regiment relieved the 49th Battalion in the Kemmel trenches from 15 until 20 February 1916, then returned to Divisional reserve at Locre. They rested for two days due to "para-typhoid" inoculation.

LETTER 87

Feb. 20th / 16
P.P.C.L.I.
L/C Bramley-Moore, 1834

My Dear Dorothy:

Many thanks for your letters. I am looking forward to the arrival of that next parcel; it hasn't turned up yet; I always acknowledge them. One does not want many cigars as one doesn't want to carry round much stuff, but just one or two or five are a great treat. I rarely smoke cigarettes, tho' occasionally I smoke one. The NCOs each got a silver plated cigarette case from Princess Patricia for Xmas; it makes a nice souvenir.

The weather has been wet and nasty. I hear you have had an extremely cold winter; I hope that has made good business for the coal mine.[110]

I shall find it difficult to find news to put in my letters as everything goes along here more or less in the same way.

We all like our rum issue; we get it early every morning when we are in the trenches. I shall want rum when I come home; I shall get a medical certificate that I suffer from nervous breakdown owing to shell shock, so that I must be allowed rum as medicine!! A lot of us soldiers will need those certificates, and I should think would be entitled to get them.

I sleep in a good many different places but I shall be glad to get home to my own bed. I think for my pleasure, when I come back, I will have William come to the door and shout "Show a leg, sixteen!" So then I will think he is the orderly corporal or sergeant and throw a boot at his head and speak to him in Greek!! Years ago your Uncle Esmonde once gave your Uncle Mostyn 10/- [*Shillings*] to

---

[110] Alwyn Bramley-Moore was vice-president of Battle River Collieries Ltd. Its president was A.S. Rosenroll of Wetaskiwin, and the district near the mine was named Rosenroll c.1915-17. C.T. Stacey of Saskatoon was the managing director. Elijah Heathcote managed the mine for several years. The mine was located about 3.5 miles east of Ohaton, Alberta, along the East Branch of the Canadian Pacific Railway out of Wetaskiwin. By October 1915 the mine employed 38 men, was partially mechanized with Ingersoll coal cutters, and produced over 100 tons of coal each day. However, by 1916, the mine went into liquidation and was taken over by the National Trust Company.

come to his carriage door when the train stopped at stations on the way from Cornwall to London and inquire, "Anything you want, my lord?" It was easy earned money, eh?

If you sent me paper, I must have lost it, so you must send more. Lots of love to all
>   from your affectionate Father
>   A B-M.

LETTER 88

Feb. 26th / 16
P.P.C.L.I.
L/C Bramley-Moore, 1834

My Dear William:

I got three letters from your Mother, Alfred and Laura the other day. Thank them for me. I am sorry to hear that it has been so terribly cold, but I hope none of your frostbites were severe.

I am writing this sitting on the floor of a dugout. The ground is the floor. I have just lit a fire in the brazier; it makes it a little smokey, but it is all right close to the ground; we have no chimney. The dugout is about 4 ft. 6 in. high and roughly 6 ft. square; four of us live in it; we have no blankets when we are in dugouts, and never take our boots off. This is rather a good one as it was built for officers, but now they have a new one.

The ground is covered with snow and it has been quite cold for this country.

The other night about 4 a.m. Corporal McCormick came to call me for duty. I was sleeping in the dugout and he looked in and called "Bramley, Bramley."[111] I thought I was up, and that Sergeant Cooper was speaking to me, and I answered "Yes, Sergeant?"[112] Then I thought that I had forgotten to post my sentries and that the Sergeant had found out, as he said "Bramley" again. I answered louder "Yes, Sergeant, I've just come from [No.1 Post], but still he kept on "Bramley, Bramley." Then I thought that he must think that I was

---

[111] Corporal J.H. McCormick, Reg. no. 410958, joined P.P.C.L.I. from 1st University Battalion on 28 July 1915. He died of wounds received near Courcelette on 15 September 1916, with the rank of Sergeant.

[112] Sergeant William Cooper, Reg. no. 1579, joined P.P.C.L.I. in August 1914. He was struck off strength to General Headquarters 14 January 1916.

asleep more than awake, and I made a desperate attempt to make him see that I was awake and get him to move on, as I wanted to dash off to attend to those sentries. Then I awoke and found that it was McCormick who had kept on saying "Bramley, Bramley" and that it was only just the right time to relieve him. I thought I had been answering out loud, but I had not been.

It is now 9:30 a.m. I have been up on and off all night and have had my tot of rum not long since, and also my breakfast. I cooked myself my slice of bacon and fried some potatoes, but there was hardly enough fat in the bacon to give me grease enough.

Lots of love to all
    from your affectionate Father
        A. B-M.

LETTER 89

March 11th / 16
P.P.C.L.I.
L/C Bramley-Moore, 1834

My Dear Alfred:

M any thanks for [your] letters. We are having our cold and nasty weather now; it has been bad now for five weeks.[113]

I have been out in No Man's Land and had a scout around; we were shot at once several times, but probably the sentry wasn't quite sure, but imagined that he saw something. Then when we stayed quiet, he would think he was mistaken. You can so easily think that a post is a man, or a tin pail or anything of a distinct black shape. It was a very nasty night, snowing and cold, and one showed up badly against the white snow.

Another morning we got a lot of shots at a German working party. They musn't have known that they could be seen from where we were, as we were a long way to one side. There were the little black figures bobbing about; they were a long way off. We shot vigorously at them; after a few rounds you could see that they had discovered they were being shot at, so there was some scuffling round;

---

[113] The P.P.C.L.I. relieved the 49th Battalion again between 3 and 8 March 1916, when it was relieved by the 28th Battalion and returned to Locre. Two days later, it went into Corps reserve at Roukloshille for training and football matches.

but some of them remained visible for some time yet, and I shot fifteen rounds more. It would be impossible to say whether we hit any; probably we did by the way they scuffled, but I fancy most of us were shooting low as we underestimated distance.

We don't often see the Germans. I look at their trenches through my periscope and they look like mountains of earth; just amazing; they must have their dugouts covered by fifteen to thirty feet of earth, so there they sit when we bombard them. They were sending trench mortars at us the other day, and every time they sent one we sent twelve shells back!! I don't know if they stopped sending the mortars earlier than they intended, as they never send very many on these ordinary occasions.

There has been big fighting at Verdun; I suppose we will have it one of these days.

Lots of love to all
    from your affectionate Father
        A. B-M.

LETTER 90

March 15th /16
L/C Bramley-Moore

My Dear Laura:

I have just packed up a small parcel with some souvenirs; I hope it will reach you safely; let me know directly you get it as it is a pleasure to know that it doesn't get lost. I think I must have lost your last parcel, and have had none since long before Xmas. You must pack extremely carefully.

I will now tell about contents of [the] parcel.

(1) The chocolate box was, as you can see, sent to us from the West Indies full of chocolate. There wasn't one for each man, but I got this box in the trenches. I used it for holding the tea ration; there are generally about four in a dugout and we have to go to the Sergeant each evening or early morning to get our rations, i.e. bread, bacon, tea, sugar, jam, etc. It is always difficult to find something to wrap the things up in and this box was very useful. It is for you; I thought it would be nice for handkerchiefs.

(2) The curtain was got from a deserted hotel; its name was the Petit Ypres Hotel, and it must have been a pleasant and merry place

before the war. The village in which it is situated is close to the trenches, and most of it is in ruins owing to shelling. I was working in front of this hotel carrying sandbags to the house next door when a shell fell two houses off. I rummaged upstairs and thought you would like this curtain; it will look different when it is washed, and is about [the] right size for [the] bathroom. I musn't tell the name of the village. The curtain is for Dorothy.

(3) The large piece of shrapnel is for Alfred; it fell in the trench just opposite my dugout. I think I told you about the time when our fire got put out just as I had finished cooking my potatoes, and another fellow was just starting to cook some bacon. It is, I think, part of the shell-casing which, when it is broken by the explosion, breaks into fragments and acts like shrapnel. They come at such speed that at times they are red hot when they hit a person. One of our fellows was hit on the chest by a piece, and it was very hot; it didn't hurt him a bit, just gave him a heavy thump and fell in front of him.

(4) The little piece is for William. As far as I can remember, its history is the same as that of the larger piece. It was got in the trenches, and either hit or was meant to hit somebody.

(5) These [types of] rings are made from shell-casings and are rather the go. But I can't vouch for its history. I don't know if you have any in Edmonton. William can have the ring if he likes.

I have a large biscuit tin here for Gladys, which came from Toronto to us, but I am not sure if I shall be able to get it posted. If I can't, I will get something else for her and send it over. But I don't promise to send souvenirs in turn; Alfred asked me for them and I must send them to those whom I think they would suit. I hope you like them and won't quarrel.

I must close and will write to Dorothy in a day or two. Madame's husband has just come home on a six days leave, and there is excitement in the house, and it looks rude to be writing. He looks very nice and well; this time he has been away six months; before that twelve months before he got leave. They have two children, girls, one eight and one two. I enclose one of the letters I got from the French boys; isn't it nice? Granny said she would send over the other.

Lots of love to all
    from your affectionate Father
        Alwyn

LETTER 91

March 18th/ 16
L/C Bramley-Moore
1834
To the Minister of Agriculture [*The Hon. Duncan Marshall*]
Edmonton Alberta

Sir:
   I trust that I may be allowed to present to the Alberta Library a book which has afforded much pleasure to many of us here and may perhaps afford equal pleasure to readers in the more peaceful atmosphere of your Library. It will be a sad day when valour lacks appreciation, and while on the one hand the perusal of the heroic deeds of another nation may tend to protect us from overestimating in too boastful a manner our national achievements, it may on the other hand stimulate us to vie with the glorious deeds we read of. War is still the final arbiter of the fate of races, and as such must be reckoned with. Be cautious before appealing to its decision, but never allow your people to lose that warlike spirit which alone can bring victory.
   Yours sincerely,
   Alwyn Bramley-Moore[114]

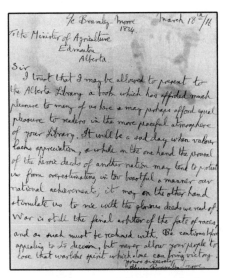

Bramley-Moore's letter attached inside the front cover of The War Drama of the Eagles.

[114] This letter was found in a pocket when Alwyn's effects were returned to his family in England. The letter and copy of Edward Fraser's book were forwarded to the Hon. Duncan Marshall by his brother, Leslie Bramley-Moore. Marshall pasted the letter inside the front cover, and handed the book over to John Blue, Provincial Librarian, on 28 July 1916. After the Second World War, Arthur Balmer Watt, Alwyn's old friend, wrote that this letter and book "constitute a memorial, that should long be prized, of the valiant patriot from whom they came."

LETTER 92

March 19th/ 16
L/C Bramley-Moore
1834

My dear Dorothy:

Your letter is a little late but I wanted to wait until I had got [*your*] parcel posted. It has now gone and I do hope it reaches you safely.

I forgot to mention in Laura's letters the gloves; I think they are very curious. They were big enough for a man, but one day when his tunic was fumigated at one of the baths, he forgot to take these gloves out of his pocket, and this is how he found them when he got his tunic back. They look as if they were meant for Tom Thumb or a dwarf. Once in a while our clothes and blankets are fumigated in order to get rid of the lice which are always attacking us. Alfred can have the gloves, if he likes them. It is difficult to send things over; let me know how you like them. I will have some other things to send if I get leave. I should have gone by now, but it was cancelled for a while, but I hear that it is starting again. Canadian mail is held up for some reason or other, for I have been some time without news.

We are moving away from this district. I may not be lucky enough to find such friendly houses where we are going. A few of us were quite treated as part of the family at one house. The husband of the lady of the house is a French sergeant and he is home now on a six day leave. They have two girls, one eight and the other two. It is funny to hear the little one say "Bramley."

I can't get the large biscuit tin over for Gladys, but something else suitable may turn up. I want you all to remember that another's good fortune doesn't mean misfortune for oneself as long as it only adds to the other's possessions and doesn't take away from ours. Learn to reason correctly; your reason separates you from the lower animals, but only if you develop it; they have reason but not the capacity for development.

Lots of love from your affectionate Father
ABM

LETTER 93

25 March 1916

Standard Military Post Card

The following instructions appear on the reverse side of the card: "Nothing is to be written on this side except the date and signature of the sender. Sentences not required may be erased. If anything else is added the post card will be destroyed."

Alwyn Bramley-Moore had crossed out all messages except, "I am quite well," "I have received your letter," and "Letter follows at first opportunity." On this date the P.P.C.L.I. relieved the 48th Battalion in the front lines at Sanctuary Wood amid heavy artillery fire on both sides.

Typical military post card, sent by Bramley-Moore on 21 November 1915.

LETTER 94

30.3.16
[*To Rev. William Bramley-Moore, 26 Russell Square, London*]

Sir:
  Sorry to have to mention that your son 1834 Cpl. Bramley-Moore received a severe head wound on the 28.3.16. Doctor says he was alive this morning & has a fighting chance to live.
  Yours in Sympathy
    E. Cooper[115]
    Platoon Sgt.
    4 Coy., P.P.C.L.I.

LETTER 95

624 Hardisty Avenue
Edmonton, Alta.
April 2nd 1916

My dear Father:
Many thanks for your letter. We are having a play. The name of it is Macbeth, and I am taking Macduff's part while Ted is Macbeth.[116]
  I have just started to wear long pants. I only wear them on Sundays yet. Ted wears them all the time now.
  The weather is fine now. The few roses that were brought in are all right. Two of them have got buds on. The others that were left outside are not uncovered yet, as the weather can not be depended upon yet.

---

[115] E. Cooper, MM, Reg. no. 1762, joined P.P.C.L.I. in August 1914. He was wounded 27 February 1915 and 19 April 1915 and struck off strength, or discharged, on 2 November 1916. He was also Mentioned in Dispatches.

[116] Frederick B. Watt (1901-1996). His father was Arthur Balmer Watt, editor of the *Edmonton Journal* from 1912 until 1945. As a boy "Teddy" Watt enlisted in the Royal Canadian Navy during the First World War by lying about his age. During the Second World War he rose to Commander and received the M.B.E. for adapting the Naval Boarding Service to improve morale among Merchant Seamen during the Battle of the Atlantic. See Commander F.B.Watt, R.C.N.(R), *In All Respects Ready: The Merchant Navy and the Battle of the Atlantic, 1940-1945*, (Scarborough: Prentice-Hall, 1985).

I most likely will go to Ashworth's this summer.[117] A regiment left here Sat. for the front. It was the 51st.

William went out to Fort Sask. with Duncan and his father to-day.[118]

I am sending a book called *Chronicles of England, France and Spain* etc. This book was written by Sir John Froissart, who lived during Edward III's time. That is the time the book deals with.[119]

Did you hear about the coins dug up at the front?

I hope you got the parcel which was sent to you.

I was at the Session Wednesday night.[120]

We are all well and I hope you are the same. I send my best wishes.

From your affectionate Son

Alfred

Alwyn Bramley-Moore as Hamlet in a student drama.

P.S. Letters are welcomed.

[*This letter was returned from the Boulogne Hospital, with the envelope marked "Deceased"*]

---

[117] The Ashworth farm was located near Kitscoty, Alberta.

[118] Duncan McLean was a friend of William's. His father was a Deputy Minister in the provincial government. The McLeans lived about half a block from the Bramley-Moore house, on 108th Street.

[119] Jean Froissart (c.1333-c.1404), French poet and historian, became court historian to the English court through the patronage of Queen Philippa. When he was sent back to France he began his *Chronicles*, which he completed between 1373 and c.1400. Froissart is best known for his *Chronicles*, which deal with the Hundred Years' War.

[120] The Legislative Session.

LETTER 96

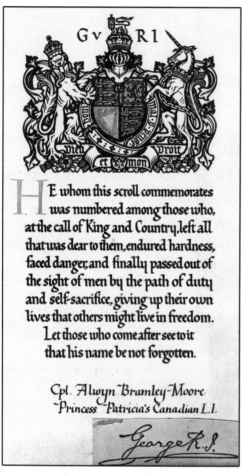

Commemorative Scroll.

4 Company PPCLI
May 9th 1916

Dear Master Bramley-Moore:

In reply to your letter which I received last night. Of course I knew your poor father very well, he being in the same section as myself. It was on March 27th that your father was wounded while he was in the first line of trenches. He was on duty going his rounds when he slightly exposed his head above the top of the parapet, when a sniper shot him; he was wearing a steel helmet at the time, and as our trenches were so close, the bullet went clean through the hat and the back of his head. He was quite conscious all the time he was being bandaged up, till he got to the dressing station. From there he was sent to a field hospital where he passed away some days later.[121] Of course I did not see him after he was taken away from the trenches.

I think that is about all. If there is anything more you wish to know or anything that I could do for you I will only be too pleased to do so. Please accept my sincere sympathy on your great loss.

Yours sincerely,
Wm. Dalby

[121] 4 April 1916.

The Path of Duty 127

Photograph of Grave No. 3076 - D 561, Boulogne Eastern Cemetery, France. Lance Corporal Alwyn Bramley-Moore was buried here on 6 April 1916.

Boulogne Eastern Cemetery. ca. 1931.

EPILOGUE

Little is known of the final days and hours of Lance Corporal Alwyn Bramley-Moore. The P.P.C.L.I. War Diary records that on 27 March 1916, the day he was shot by a German sniper, there was heavy shelling heard for about three hours in the direction of St. Eloi during the early morning. Heavy shelling was heard again in the early afternoon. "Otherwise," the Diary notes, "quiet on this front."

The next day the Regiment was relieved by the 9th Battalion, during a very dark night in a driving snow storm. While his companions were resting in reserve, Bramley-Moore had been removed to the Boulogne Hospital. He died there on 4 April 1916.

Sniping along this front remained a deadly feature of trench life during April, taking its steady toll. When the Patricias were relieved by the 60th Battalion on 20 April 1916, the War Diary recorded that during its most recent tour 16 men had been killed and 45 wounded. As the train took Bramley-Moore's mates back to Brandhoek, where they occupied a rest camp, the names of the dead were not recorded, but were temporarily swallowed up by the carnage of the Great War.

In 1955 Brigadier A. Hamilton Gault, Alwyn's old commanding officer, wrote to Dr. Alfred Bramley-Moore, Alwyn's brother. Gault admitted that he "had no realisation of his outstanding work for the Province of Alberta" until that year. Unconsciously echoing Bramley-Moore's words, he wrote that (it) "is the awful ... truth of war that the young and promising are always the ones to pay the supreme penalty for their patriotism while others less fit are left to carry on the business of life." Alluding to the note found in his copy of *War Drama of the Eagles*, Gault concluded "the heroic words of his letter are indeed a great memorial to the part he played in life."

BIOGRAPHICAL AFTERWORD

Alfred

Alfred Gordon Bramley-Moore trained as a lawyer. After being admitted to the Bar in Alberta, he worked for Credit Foncier. Alfred remained their legal council until his retirement. Following retirement, he went into private practice. Alfred always was keenly interested in history and in politics. He also was a member of the Rifle Club, winning many trophies. He remained an avid hunter for many years. Alfred died on 27 August 1981.

Laura

Gladys Bramley-Moore recalls that although her sister Laura was born in Ontario (14 January 1902) and died in British Columbia, "she was a true Albertan." She spent much of her life working in the Legislature as an accountant. She later became director of one of the branches in the Treasury Department. Her interests included the Business and Professional Women's Association, of which she became President. She also was Worthy Matron of the Order of the Eastern Star. Laura died on 8 January 1997.

Dorothy

Dorothy (b. 20 February 1904) became a teacher, starting her career in rural districts before working for the Edmonton Public Schools. She loved to travel, spending a year on exchange in St. Thomas, Ontario, and two years in Baden Baden, Germany, with the Department of National Defence. She later was appointed Assistant Principal at Queen Mary Park School in Edmonton. She loved to travel

The Bramley-Moore sisters travelled to Boulogne to see their father's grave in 1931.

throughout her life, and her sister, Gladys, recalls that as soon as one trip was planned she was busy reading and starting plans for the next one. Dorothy died on 8 October 1993.

William

William Bramley-Moore (b. 4 May 1906), like his father, would serve his country in uniform during the Second World War. He graduated in medicine from the University of Alberta in 1931, and was a general practitioner in Jasper, Alberta, and Blue River, British Columbia until the outbreak of war in September 1939. He enlisted in Calgary with the 8th Field Ambulance, Canadian Army Medical Corps. After service with the Canadian Corps Headquarters, William returned to Canada in 1943 to become the first Medical Officer to attend the Staff Officers Training Course for all aspects of combat, at Kingston, Ontario. The following year he was selected as one of a small contingent of Canadian officers sent to Burma to study jungle warfare. By 1945, William was Chief Instructor at Camp Borden, at A22, the C.A.M.C. Medical Training Centre. In 1946, he became Registrar for the Alberta College of Physicians and Surgeons, a position which he would hold for 21 years. William was named President of the Canadian Medical Council in 1965. A park in the Riverbend area of Edmonton was named in his honour in 1984. William died on 29 March 1976.

Nellie Bramley-Moore with her sons Alfred (left) and William, in Edmonton during the Second World War

Gladys

Gladys Bramley-Moore (b. 2 June 1909) chose education as a career, like her sister, Dorothy. She recalls that after doing her time in the country schools, she came to Edmonton to teach. Gladys was Assistant Principal at Prince Charles School for nineteen years before her retirement. She also spent a year on exchange in Sarnia, Ontario, near her family's first farm in Sombra. During the Second World War she worked in a munitions plant in Ajax, Ontario. Like her sisters, Gladys enjoys travel, and spent many holidays skiing at Mount Temple, Skoki Lodge and Jasper National Park.

END NOTES

INTRODUCTION: "ALBERTA, FIRST, LAST AND FOREVER"

[1] See Letter 34 (17 July 1915).

[2] London Court Directory, 1877; St. George's, Bloomsbury Census (1881), Public Records Office (PRO) RG 11/320, pp. 38-39; St. George's, Bloomsbury Census (1891), PRO, RG 12/209, p. 26.

[3] E. Clive Rouse and Rev. J. Gordon Harrison, *Gerrards Cross and its Parish Church* (Tonbridge, Kent: Tonbridge Printers Limited, 1959).

[4] The Rev. Isaac Barr promoted settlement on a large tract of land located west of Maidstone in 1902, and in March 1903 he brought about two thousand English "colonists" to Canada. This group arrived in Saskatoon on 17 April 1903, where they spent two weeks forming a wagon train which took them further west to their land. Internal bickering and lack of experience plagued the colonists from the beginning. Rev. George Lloyd took over the enterprise, and the main town in the district was named for him in July 1903.

[5] Fred A. Acland, "Alberta, 1906," *Alberta History*, 28:1 (Winter 1980): 6-20.

[6] *Ibid.*

[7] Edmonton *Bulletin*, 25 February, 1910; *Edmonton Journal*, 1 March, 1910.

[8] *Calgary Herald*, 18 November, 1910; Edmonton *Bulletin*, 22 November, 1910; Edmonton *Bulletin*, 3 December, 1910; Edmonton *Bulletin*, 15 December, 1910.

[9] D.R. Babcock, *A Gentleman of Strathcona Alexander Cameron Rutherford*. Edmonton: University of Calgary Press, Friends of Rutherford House, 1989.

[10] Alwyn Bramley-Moore, *Canada and Her Colonies, or Home Rule for Alberta*. London: W. Stewart & Co., 1911.

[11] *Edmonton Journal*, 4-6 June, 1980.

[12] Bramley-Moore, *Canada and Her Colonies*, p.174.

[13] *Ibid.*, p. 185.

[14] Bramley-Moore, unpublished manuscript.

[15] *Ibid.*

[16] *Ibid.*

[17] *Ibid.*

[18] Major James Robert Lowery operated a real estate business in Edmonton at the time, and later was the founder of the Home Oil Company. Lowery served with the 49th Battalion, C.E.F. during the war, and was re-elected for Alexandra on 7 June 1917 while serving overseas, shortly after being wounded at Vimy Ridge.

[19] Alix *Free Press*, 4 April, 1913.

[20] Provincial Archives of Alberta, Energy Resources Conservation Board Records, 77.237/302. See Letter 87 (20 February, 1916).

[21] Ministry of Defence, Military Service Records, Corporal Alwyn Bramley-Moore, 179, Royal Fusiliers.

[22] National Archives of Canada, Record Group 24, Volume 19,056/DND (1451-603/Pt.1(vol.1). See Letters 59 and 61 (15 November, 1915 and 20 November 1915).

Index

Acland, Fred A., x
Adair, Joseph W., 12, 36, 55, 84, 9n, 12n, 13n
Adamson, Captain Agar, v, xxi, xxii, 58n, 61n, 106n
Aesop's Fables, 66, 71, 93
Aksenoff, Ivan Dmitrich, 25, 39, 25n
Alberta, viii, xi, xii, xiii, xiv, xv, xvi, xx, 13-4, 16, 41, 43, 59, 77, 92, 129
Alberta and Great Waterways Railway, xi, xii
Alberta and Great Waterways Railway debate, xi, xii
Alberta Legislature Library, 79, 88, 121, 79n
alcohol, 69
Alexandra Constituency, xi, xviii
Anderson, Lt. Col. Peter, 38, 44, 115, 38n
Arabic, S.S., 66, 70, 66n
Ashworth family, 36, 44, 125, 36n, 125n
Australians, 4, 11
Austrians, 44

bands, 5, 7, 27, 74, 74n, 84n
Barr Colony, x, 62, 2n, 36n, 62n
barracks, 5-6, 20, 52
Battalions: 1st University Battalion, 103n, 117n; 2nd University Battalion, 87n; 3rd Battalion C.E.F., 38n; 4th Battalion C.E.F., 106n; 9th Battalion C.E.F., 129, 38n; 11th Reserve Battalion, xix ; 17th Battalion C.E.F., 80n, 80n; 23rd Service Battalion Royal Fusiliers [1st Sportsman's], 10; 28th Battalion C.E.F., 118n; 31st Battalion C.E.F., 109n; 42nd Battalion C.E.F., 100n, 107n; 48th Battalion C.E.F., 123; 49th Battalion C.E.F., 109, 100n, 109n, 115n, 118n; 60th Battalion C.E.F., 129
Battle River Collieries, xix, 28n, 116n
Before Adam, Jack London, 2-4, 19, 27, 2n
Bennett, Lt. C.M., 103, 103n
Bennett, George, 47n
Bennett, Richard B., xi, xix, 42, 46-9, 42n, 47n
billets, 62, 73, 79, 86, 91, 93-4, 98-100, 104, 122, 79n

Black, W.P., 32
Blue, John, 121n
Blue Bird: A Fairy Play in Six Acts, The, Maurice Maeterlinck, 25, 58, 60, 25n
Bonar Law, Andrew, 42n
books, 1, 3, 12, 18, 21, 25, 29, 37, 41, 43, 56, 58, 64, 69-72, 86, 95, 100, 108, 125
Borden, Prime Minister Sir Robert, xix, 42, 42n, 47n
Boulogne, viii, 125, 129, 8n, 84n
Boves, 68n
Boyle, J.R., xi, xiii
Bramley-Moore, A.J., 9
Bramley-Moore, Alfred [brother], xix, 39, 41, 103-4, 129, 72n, 104n
Bramley-Moore, Alfred [son], v, viii, 1, 3, 36, 55, 71, 107, 120, 122, 124-5, 130, 28n, 80n, 91n
Bramley-Moore, Alwyn: birth and education, x; immigration, xi; political career, xii-xiv; *Canada and Her Colonies*, xiv-xvii; social thought, xvii-xix; business interests, xix-xx; sworn in with P.P.C.L.I., 51; joins E Company, Sportsman's Battalion, 40; orderly corporal, 93, 99; birthday, 41; health, 11, 19-21, 23, 30, 37, 51, 106-7, 110-11; grows moustache, 5, 32; Greek and Roman history, views, 16, 18, 69, 90, 111; made Lance-Corporal, 24, 52; political views, 13-16; quarantined, 29-31, 30n; in casualty hut, 47; training, 25-8, 34-5; death, ix, 126
Bramley-Moore, Dorothy, 32, 42, 45, 49, 63, 120, 130-1, 8n, 87n
Bramley-Moore, Ella Bradshaw Jordan ["Granny"], ix, 8, 10, 28, 31, 42, 48, 63, 71, 74, 98, 102, 104, 120
Bramley-Moore, Eva, 1, 71, 1n
Bramley-Moore, Gladys, 23, 35, 60, 62-3, 66, 73-4, 87, 89, 93, 95, 101-2, 107, 120, 122, 132, 8n, 18n, 19n, 37n, 45n, 72n
Bramley-Moore, John, 8
Bramley-Moore, Laura, 2, 17, 24, 27, 31, 37, 51, 63, 71, 87, 130, 8n, 87n
Bramley-Moore, Leslie, 7, 11, 13, 11n
Bramley-Moore, Mostyn, 11, 104, 116-17, 11n, 121n

136

Bramley-Moore, Nellie Grieve, ix, 1, 7-9, 12, 17, 20, 29, 35, 43, 51, 56, 75, 87, 95, 98, 100, 102, 111, 117, 45n, 60n; 72n
Bramley-Moore, Swinfen, 41
Bramley-Moore, William, 1, 23, 35, 71, 87, 96-8, 101-4, 116, 120, 125, 131, 26n, 36n, 72n, 125n
Bramley-Moore, Rev. William Joseph, ix, 8, 124
Brandhoek, 129
Brigades: 7th Canadian Infantry Brigade, 3rd Canadian Division, 100n 109n; 80th Brigade, 27th Division, B.E.F., 52n, 74n
"British Grenadiers," regimental march, 5
bugle calls, 6, 20
Buller, Col. H.C., 96n, 97n
Bulletin, Edmonton, ix, 12n
Bulyea, Lieutenant-Governor George H.V., xi

Caistre, 84n
Calgary Eye-Opener, 99, 99n
Cambridgeshire Regiment, 67n
camps, military, 1, 5, 30-1, 35, 38-9, 41, 46, 49, 67, 82, 105-6, 19n, 39n
Camp Borden, 131
Canada and Her Colonies, or Home Rule for Alberta, viii, xiii, xiv
Canadians, 3-4, 9, 16, 19, 29, 33-4, 39, 42-3, 49, 74, 84, 19n, 29n, 34n, 109n
Capital, Edmonton, 9, 9n
Cappy, 55n
censors, censored material, 67, 83, 83n
children, childhood, 9, 13, 16, 27, 43, 54-5, 58-60, 74-5, 81-2, 94, 113, 19n
Christianity, xvi, xvii, xviii, 3-4, 25-6, 90, 112-14, 25n, 70n
Christie, Doug, 91, 105, 91n
Christmas, 92-4, 96, 99-104, 116, 119
Christmas story, 80-83
Churchill, John, Duke of Marlborough, 37, 37n
Cold Lake, xix, 28, 36, 41, 46-7, 49, 62, 49n
colours, trooping, 96-7, 97n
Cooper, Sergeant E., 124, 124n
Cooper, Sergeant William, 117, 117n

cooking, cookhouses, 6-7, 20-1, 65, 93-4, 118
Couchee, Judith, 112
Cowley, Lt., 61, 61n
Cushing, William H., xi
Cutler, Jane E., ix, 7-8, 8n

Dalby, Private William, 80, 89-90, 98, 126, 80n
De Balinhard, Lt., 61, 61n
discipline, 20-2, 25, 36, 44, 48, 53-4, 67, 85-6, 100
divisional drill, 35
Divisions, Canadian: 1st Canadian Division, 19n, 34n; 2nd Canadian Division, 29n, 39n; 3rd Canadian Division, 109n.
dugouts, 60, 65, 82, 108, 117, 119, 61n
drill, 5-7, 11, 17, 22-3, 32-4, 36, 42-3, 46-7, 52, 67, 71, 78, 87

Eclusier, 55n
Edmonton, viii, x, xi, xii, xiii, xvi, xix, 3, 5, 13-14, 56, 85, 115, 130-32, 9n, 12n, 13n, 38n, 105n, 109n
Edmonton, flood of 1915, 45, 45n
Edmonton Fusiliers, 38n
Edmonton Journal, ix, xiv, 9, 9n, 124n
Edmonton Printing and Publishing Company, 12
education, see "school classes."
Edwards, Robert ["Bob"] Chambers, 99, 99n
Empire Theatre, Edmonton, 105, 105n
England, 22, 37, 54, 67, 71, 86, 92, 95, 105, 110, 8n, 19n, 29n, 42n, 49n
English immigrants, x, 9, 2n
Essex, 1, 46

Fabian Society, xvi
Ferrières, 68n
flags, 79
Flêtre, 88, 84n, 103n, 106n, 107n
Flixecourt, 79n
France, French, 8, 19, 52, 60, 67, 71, 74, 77-8, 104, 122, 19n
French, Field Marshal Sir John, 4
Frezenberg, battle, 80n, 83n
friends, 4, 13, 41, 53, 55, 57-8, 63, 98
Frise, 59n

137

Froissy, 55n
"Front," 3, 10-11, 16, 25, 31, 35-6, 42-3, 46-7, 49, 52, 55, 57-8, 60, 63, 80, 84, 97-8, 123, 125, 129, 59n, 80n, 106n
Froude, James Anthony, 29, 29n

games, 1, 5, 19, 24, 44, 54, 56, 72, 86, 99, 99n
gas, 33, 111, 34n
Gault, Major A. Hamilton, xix, 78, 97, 100, 129, 78n
Gee, Bernard, 36, 36n
General Uniformity, 86
Germans, 1, 4, 9, 22, 25, 31, 37, 42-5, 48, 60, 62, 65-9, 73, 75-6, 80, 82, 85-6, 91, 96, 108, 111-12, 115, 118-19, 129-30, 34n, 58n, 61n, 101n
Gilchrist family, 108-9, 109n
Ginn, Robert Wesley, xix
Globe, Toronto, x
Grenville, Sir Richard, 29, 29n
Grey Towers Barracks, Hornchurch, Essex, 3, 21
Guillancourt, 54n

Hallowe'en, 85
Halma, game, 99, 99n
Harris, Clifford, 30, 106, 30n
Harris, Aunt Milly, 30, 30n
Harris, Ruth, 30, 30n
Hazebrouck, 54n, 84n
Heathcote, Elijah, 28, 36, 43, 28n, 116n
Hesperian, S.S., 51, 66, 70, 51n, 66n
Hindenberg, 73
history, 26, 37, 39, 44, 68-9, 90, 95, 111-12, 19n
Hopkins, Marshall Willard, xix, 17, 38, 95, 104, 17n
Horatius, see "Lays of Ancient Rome."
Hornchurch, Essex, 1, 7, 47, 49
hunting, 41, 55, 81
huts, life in, 2, 6, 8, 19-20, 23, 25, 40-2, 47, 55n
Hyde Park, 7

Ingoldsby Legends, The, Thomas Ingoldsby, 82, 82n
inoculations, 115, 115n

"Jack Johnsons," 33, 33n
"Jackdaw of Rheims," see *Ingoldsby Legends*.
Jamieson, Lt. Col. Frederick C., 41, 41n
Johnson family, 2, 39-40, 95, 115
Johnson, Gladys, 114-15, 114n
Jones, Major Stanley L., xxii, 59n, 61n, 61n, 68n, 79n, 84n, 97n
Jordan, Leighton, 100, 100n

Kemmel trenches, 100n, 106n, 109n, 115n
Kinloch, Mary Anne, 72n
Kirkpatrick, Reggie, 28, 28n
Kitchener, Field Marshal Earl H.H., 4
Kitchener Kit, 100
Kitscoty, 49, 103, 28n, 36n, 103n, 109n, 125n

La Clyte, 100n
Laurier, Sir Wilfrid, xv, xvi
Lays of Ancient Rome, Thomas Babington Macauley, 77, 77n
lice, 110, 122
Lloydminster, x, xix, 62, 109, 115, 62n, 114n
Locre, 109n, 115n, 118n
London, 1, 5, 7, 12, 28, 37-8, 51, 64, 117, 30n
luck, 10-1, 31, 60, 102, 122
Lucy, Aunt, 38, 48
Lyster, N.C., xviii

McCormick, Corporal J.H., 117-8, 117n
McIsaac, Private F., 80, 89-90, 98, 103, 80n
McKay Avenue School, 37n, 45n
McLean, Duncan, 125, 125n
McNamara family, 71, 71n
McQueen, Lance Corporal Alex R., 86-7, 87n
Macauley, Thomas Babington, 77n
machine guns, 58n
marching, route marches, 1-2, 34, 36-7, 52, 68, 85, 91, 102, 105, 107, 109, 52n, 54n, 55n, 68n, 74n, 79n, 106n, 109n
Marshall, Hon. Duncan, 121, 121n
Maxim machine gun, 35, 59
Meredith, George, 14, 14n

Millen, A., 32
Miller, Hiram, 108, 108n
Minnie, 37, 72, 112, 72n
Mont des Cats, sports day, 109n
Morcourt, 67, 67n
Morgan, J. Pierpont, xi
Mrs. Grundy, 85
mud, 24, 71, 91, 98, 100, 102-3, 105-6
Muhlbach, L., 68, 111, 68n, 69n
Munchausen, Baron, 95, 95n

Napoleon, 83
natural resources, xiii, xiv
Neale, Corporal G., 98, 98n
Neuve Chapelle, battle, 80, 80n
New Year, 9, 12-16, 84, 927, 102-3, 103n
newspapers, clippings, 3, 13-16, 45, 54, 87, 94-96, 12n, 99n
Nicholson, George W.L., 29n, 39n, 83n
No Man's Land, 118

officers, 10, 24, 26, 28, 30, 38, 42, 46-7, 61, 74, 115, 117
Ohaton, Alberta, xix, 116n
Oliver, Frank, xiii

patriotism, 3, 6, 9, 11, 77, 95
Patterson, Private B., 80-84, 80n
periscopes, in trenches, 96, 108, 115, 119
Perley, Sir George, 42n
Petit Ypres Hotel, 119
post cards, 9, 17, 35, 57, 59, 81, 97, 100, 123
Princess Patricia, Christmas gifts, 116
Princess Patricia's Canadian Light Infantry, ii, iii, v, viii, xv, xix, xxi, 16, 29, 39-40, 42, 51, 53, 78, 80, 88; 96-7, 123, 129, 47n, 51n, 52n, 54n, 67n, ff66, 79n, 80n, 83n, 103n, 107n, 109n, 118n
prohibition, 92, 116, 92n
Puffer, William F., xviii

quilt ["William's Quilt"], 71, 74, 84, 87, 101, 72n

rats, 60, 104, 58n, 106n
religion, xvii-xix, 25-6, 56, 73, 90, 93, 112, 114

Romford, 6, 32, 51
Rosenroll, A.S., xix, 116n
Rouen, 52
Rougemont, Michel Nicolas Balisson de, 95, 95n
Roukloshille, 118n
Royal Canadian Regiment, 109, 100n, 109n
Royal Fusiliers [Sportsman's Battalion], xix, 7, 10, 46, 53, 86
"Rule Britannia," 27
rum rations, 92-3, 116, 118
rumours, 22-3, 46, 68, 115, 68n
Russians, 37, 44-7, 101n
Russell, Bertrand, xvi
Russell Square [No. 26], 5, 31, 38, 40, 49, 124, 1n, 8n
Rutherford, Premier Alexander C., xi, xii, xiii, xviii

St. Eloi, battles, 80, 80n
Salisbury Plain, 19, 19n, 39n
Sarnia, Ontario, ix, 132, 60n
Saskatoon, v, x, xix, 62, 2n, 62n, 116n
school classes, 2, 23, 32, 37, 43-4, 49, 59-60, 66, 71, 90, 93, 102
Serbia, 11, 59, 74, 78, 101, 68n, 101n
separation allowance, 1, 6, 26, 43, 51
Shakespeare, 43, 71
Shaw, G.B., 70, 70n
Shorncliffe Camp, 39, 51, 95, 39n, 51n
Sidmouth, 8
Sifton, Premier Arthur L., viii, xii, xiii, 92n
Smiles, Samuel, 18, 18n
snipers, iii, viii, 62, 66-7, 75, 77, 96, 108, 115, 118-19, 126, 129, 115n
Sombra, Ontario, ix, 69, 132, 60n, 72n, 78n
South African War, 71, 72n, 104n
souvenirs, 34, 80-3, 89, 96-7, 100, 108, 116, 119, 120
sports, football matches, 74, 98, 109, 109n, 118n
Stacey. C.T., xix, 116n

"Tale of Ivan the Fool," 40, 40n
Tennyson, Alfred, Lord, 29, 29n

Tidworth Barracks, England, xix
"Tipperary," 27
Tolstoy, Leo, 39, 25n, 40n
Town Topics, 9, 13, 42, 9n, 12n
Tredway, Sylvester, 13n
trenches, 4, 6, 11-12, 16, 22, 46, 53-4, 60-3, 65-8, 71, 75, 77-8, 84-6, 89, 91-2, 96, 98, 101-2, 104-6, 108-9, 115, 119-20, 126, 129, 55n, 58n, 61n, 68n, 83n, 100n, 106n, 109n, 115n
trench mortars, shelling, 67, 73, 101-2, 106, 108, 119

uniforms, gear, 7, 32-3, 51, 83, 85-6, 100, 110
university recruits, Alberta, 99

valentines, 23-4
Verdun, 119
Vermilion Constituency, xi
Vermilion and Cold Lake Company, xix
Victoria Constituency, 2n

Victoria High School, 53, 37n

Walker, Francis A., 2, 84, 106, 115, 2n
War Drama of the Eagles, Edward Fraser, 79, 129, 79n, 88n, 121n
warfare, 3, 8-12, 17, 22, 27, 29, 31, 36-7, 39-42, 44-6, 48-9, 54-5, 70, 95-6, 121, 129, 49n
Warleigh Barracks, 20
Watt, Arthur Balmer, ix, 9n, 121n, 124n
Watt, Frederick Balmer, 61, 124, 124n
Webb, Beatrice, xvi
Wells, H.G., xv
Western Weekly, 13-16, 20, 25, 31, 12n, 13n
"whizz-bangs," 65, 102-3, 61n, 65n
women, 11, 41, 55-7, 19n
Wood Farm, Dranoutre, 106n, 107n

Yorkshire, 35

Zeppelin raids, 12, 39